ated
d on
each.

ic Type.

*Flower Arranging
and Flower Festivals
in Church*

Flower Arranging & Flower Festivals in Church

GRIZELDA MAURICE

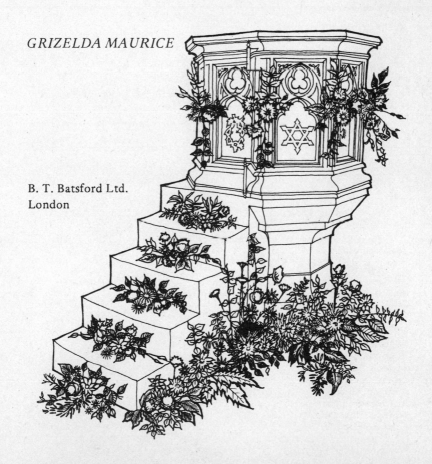

B. T. Batsford Ltd.
London

For Spencer

Typeset by Tek-Art Ltd, London SE20
and printed in Great Britain by
Butler & Tanner Ltd
Frome, Somerset
for the publishers
B. T. Batsford Ltd.
4 Fitzhardinge Street
London W1H 0AH

Contents

Acknowledgments

I am very grateful to all those who have helped me in the preparation
of this book. The illustrations are a very important part of it and I
thank the Reverend Derek E. Cook, Vicar of St John Baptist, Stanbridge,
Bedfordshire, and his son Jeremy for the photographs taken at the
Flower Festival there; Mr Andrew Harrison for the colour photograph taken at the Flower Festival at St John Baptist, Great Gaddesden,
Hertfordshire; Mr Terry Ryder who with his usual skill and patience
took the rest of the photographs; and Mr Bruce Hyatt who did all the
drawings and greatly helped to add clarity to the text. Some of the
flower festival arrangements shown are not my own and I am glad to be
able to pay tribute to the skill and care of those responsible for them
particularly Mrs Betty Escombe, Mrs Pat Taylor and Mrs Eleanor
Massey.

I am indebted to the Very Reverend Peter Moore, Dean of the Cathedral and Abbey Church of St Albans, for permission to use photographs
of the 1977 Flower Festival and to illustrate the construction equipment used in the Abbey; and to the Reverend Doctor Paul Bradshaw,
Vicar of St Leonard, Flamstead, Hertfordshire, for advice on liturgical
and other matters. I am also grateful to Mr Cook, Doctor Bradshaw, the
Reverend Patrick Evans, Vicar of Great Gaddesden, and the Reverend
John Shepherd, Rector of St Mary Magdalene, Whipsnade, Bedfordshire,
for allowing me to use photographs taken in their respective churches.
I have had much valuable assistance from the St Albans Abbey Flower
Guild, particularly from Mrs Margaret Freeman, who allowed me to use
the Guild's model form of instructions for its members, Mrs Elizabeth
Ward Lilley, and Mrs Judith Holroyd.

I am grateful to Mrs Margaret Gall for her help in reading the proofs
and to my publishers for the help and advice which they have given me.
Most of all I thank my husband for constant encouragements and for
typing the manuscript.

G.M.
St Albans 1982

List of Illustrations

Introduction

I can never be sufficiently grateful for the fact that my initial florist's training has enabled me to work with flowers for over 30 years. During this time my work has taken me to churches of infinite variety both of age and of architecture and each one has been a challenge from which some new lesson has been learned. During the last 15 years I have particularly specialized in flower festival work, both as a helper and as an artistic director. In this field I have been privileged to work with brilliant flower arrangers. Through their inspiration and skill my own vision of flower decorating in churches has increased enormously.

The aim of this book is to share the knowledge which I have gained with those who want to extend their own ideas when arranging flowers in churches.

This book is of course intended to be appropriate to all denominations, but as a matter of convenience I have used terms associated with the Church of England.

1
The Flower Guild

In most churches flowers are used as a means of decoration throughout the greater part of the year. To ensure that there are flowers at all times when it is appropriate to have them, it is wise to form a flower guild, that is to say, a team of people who are prepared to take turns in arranging the flowers week by week and, which is just as important, to maintain them. There is nothing sadder than to visit a church mid-week and to be greeted with dead flowers.

In a church which has no existing flower rota the first step in organizing a guild is to elect a chairman, whose task it will be to start up the guild and ensure that it works in an orderly way. The ideal person to have is one who knows the building well, understands the kind of flower arrangements best suited to its style, and is knowledgeable about the conditioning of flower material. It is even more important that she should have the ability and patience to inspire and encourage new flower arrangers to join her team, as well as more experienced flower decorators.

The method used to choose a chairman varies slightly from church to church. In a cathedral the dean is responsible for looking after the building and the arrangement of the services. Generally he likes to decide where there are to be flowers and will seek as chairman someone from the congregation upon whom he can rely to run the guild in a sympathetic and efficient way. In parish churches of the Church of England the chairman will be chosen by the incumbent, but, particularly if he is new to the parish, he may ask the advice of the Parochial Church Council. In the Roman Catholic Church the choice will usually lie with the parish priest, and in non-conformist churches with the minister or the governing body of the local congregation. I speak of 'guild' as this is a convenient term; but in many churches 'flower rota' is used to signify the same sort of organization.

Once the guild is working well a retiring chairman is generally replaced by another guild member who seems to be the natural successor. In most big churches the chairman usually takes the job for three years. When the chairman has been chosen it is up to her to recruit her team.

The guild must always aim for very high standards — but must at the same time be compassionate if a new and inexperienced member is slow in reaching the goal. Encouragement and practical help will soon produce confidence and ability. I am not happy about churches where one person alone undertakes all the flower arrangements and allows no-one else to take an active part. If she leaves the district or is away ill, a substitute taking over for the first time may well be too frightened to enjoy her new job! It must be remembered too that most parishes have people who would like to take part in arranging the flowers but are too nervous to offer their help. These need to be drawn into the guild. If the guild is looking for new members, a cry for help on a special occasion is likely to bring volunteers and the opportunity is provided to recruit those with talent on a permanent basis. It is also worthwhile asking individuals who are not very regular church attenders but like arranging flowers. In this way they may become interested in the church, especially if the guild is friendly and welcoming. Many people are shy of offering help but will gladly help if specifically asked.

The size of the guild depends upon the number of flower arrangements which the church has each week. A factor to take into account is whether the building is open all day during the week, because in that case more care will have to be given to the flowers. (Alas! due to vandalism many churches are now only open for Sunday services.) Cathedrals are likely to have 10-14 arrangements at all times, including some big pedestal arrangements, and will therefore require about 70 members in the guild. A large parish church will need 30-40 members, and small churches 10-20, depending to some extent on how often they are open.

In Anglican and Roman Catholic churches it is customary not to have flowers during Advent — which extends over the four Sundays before Christmas — and Lent, the period from Ash Wednesday to Easter Eve of which the 40 weekdays are traditionally devoted to fasting and penitence in commemoration of Christ in the wilderness. On the other hand there are other denominations which have flowers every Sunday throughout the year. In those churches which do not have flowers during Advent and Lent, these periods are available to the members of the flower guild for cleaning their vases and flower cupboards, laundering the dust-sheets, and generally doing the chores which a busy flower year makes otherwise impossible! These are times, too, which provide a chance to check up on the equipment. It is astonishing how vases disappear, pedestals get loaned out and not always returned, and cones are totally lost without trace! It is, I feel, the chairman's responsibility to see that missing equipment is replaced, if necessary by drawing on the flower guild fund.

If the church is a large one, I suggest that the chairman ought to move the members of the guild about, for if one person always does one particular arrangement a situation may be reached in which it almost 'belongs' to her and umbrage is taken if anyone else dares to do it! I remember an occasion when I was directing a flower festival and I wanted a garland in a particular area. I was told very firmly, 'No, Mrs Smith wouldn't like that. She always arranges her pedestal there!' If the flower arrangers are moved about, sometimes doing pedestals and some-times small vases, the chairman is given a chance to assess her really skilled people, and they can then be used to advantage for special occasions. Some churches have small niches or little tables, and these provide a good way of keeping older and perhaps frail members active in the work of the guild.

Once the chairman has collected a team it is a friendly idea if all meet together for coffee — perhaps in the church itself — to learn who their fellow arrangers are. The chairman can then explain exactly what their duties are and show them the lay-out of the church — where the flower cupboard is, etc, and she can also tell them exactly what con-ditioning of flowers entails. A verbal explanation of duties is not, however, enough. They must be clearly set down in writing, and there must also be a rota so that each member of the guild knows exactly when she is required. A copy of the rota and the list of duties must be displayed in a prominent place, e.g. on the flower arrangers' cupboard or the church notice board.

Mrs Freeman of St Alban's Abbey Flower Guild has a splendid form in which the Guild's organization is explained and the duties of the members are set out. It was compiled many years ago and because it is so clear I have with her permission modelled upon it the following form of instructions to be given to flower guild members. It is intended that it should be signed by the chairman.

ORGANIZATION OF THE FLOWER GUILD

Purpose
The purpose of church flowers is to glorify God by enhancing the beauty of the building. We aim at providing natural-looking arrangements which are kept in immaculate condition throughout the week.

The rota
The rota is compiled once a year and is distributed during Lent. If you cannot manage your dates on the rota, please change with someone else or let me know. If you want to arrange flowers on a special date, please let me know by Christmas. When there are special services and weddings, people normally arranging in that week will be notified.

Arrangements and their care

(1) Arrangements to be finished and cleared by 5 pm during the week and 11 am on Saturday.
(2) Clear previous arrangements and clean the containers. This includes cones if used. Put old unsuitable *Oasis** in the dustbin and tip other rubbish out of the dust-sheet into the incinerator.
(3) If you use *Oasis*, please do not put it on top of pin-holders. There are special *Oasis* holders with only long pins.
(4) Use only clean water.
(5) Any usable flowers left over from your arrangement should be put in a bucket by the flower cupboard.
(6) Remember to top up and spray flowers when you have finished your arrangement. Flowers can take up quite half the water in a container while the arrangement is being done.
(7) Sweep and mop thoroughly after finishing your flowers and put away your equipment in the right place. Store pin-holders *pins down*. Fold up dust-sheets and put them away in the cupboard. If still wet, dry out first.
(8) Daily care. Please check your flowers during the week. If you are unable to do this, let me know.
(9) Expenditure. It is hoped that garden flowers will be used if possible. If for a special occasion you need to buy flowers, please let me know and I will tell you what the allowance is and give the bill to the Treasurer.
(10) Storage of equipment. All dust-sheets, watering cans, dustpans and brushes, spare cones, chicken wire, *Oasis*, pin-holders, small containers, etc, should be put in the flower arrangers' cupboard; pedestals and large containers in the vestry [or some other suitable place].

Committee meetings
We generally meet as a guild twice a year. Notice of meetings will be given a fortnight in advance.
    I hope that this information will be of use to members. If you have any problems, please do not hesitate to telephone me.

(*Signed. Address and telephone number*)

If a church — even a very small one — takes these instructions as a guide, the flower rota should work well, and a happy, flourishing guild result. Working in churches during flower festivals I have noticed that those which have properly organized flower guilds always have an efficiently working team and have the basic mechanics and the conditioning of flowers well prepared in advance.

Most flower guilds have a fund on which to draw for special occasions, but ordinarily members are encouraged to use garden flowers and foliage and to go out to the hedgerows. Most cathedrals and large churches are allocated a yearly sum by the finance committee and this is augmented by fund-raisers such as coffee mornings and plant sales. For example, the St Alban's Abbey Flower Guild holds a wonderful

*A trade name.

plant sale in the autumn in the form of a 'bring and buy'. This is perfectly splendid. It raises a lot of money and it provides a great opportunity to increase the growing of interesting plants for both churches and gardens. People bring and buy from a great distance. Small churches often prefer to be entirely self-supporting, organizing their own fund-raisers, and receiving donations from weddings and christenings. The fund is always under the chairman's control and flower arrangers requiring money apply to her with a receipt for flowers purchased.

2

Containers

The term 'container' is used by flower arrangers to embrace any utensil which holds flowers or *Oasis* and can therefore be used for flower arrangements. In this chapter, pedestals and constructions are also covered, because they are ancillary to the use of containers.

In the old days arrangers were much less adventurous in the use of containers than they are to-day, limiting themselves to brass or occasionally cut-glass vases, while in country churches one would sometimes see jam jars standing about, completely uncamouflaged. Now, I am happy to say, there is a much more imaginative approach and anything is permissible, from kitchen casseroles to priceless silver goblets.

Jumble sales and white elephant stalls are very good sources for containers: but it is important not to get too carried away by textures or colour. What is necessary in a container is that it should have a good wide top and be well balanced. Some urn-type vases have narrow bases. When filled with flowers the whole thing overturns, which is a disaster!

Another good source for containers for churches is the church members' flower and kitchen cupboards. A plea by the flower guild may encourage members to empty their cupboards and give their less used containers to the church. Not only casseroles but also pâte dishes, tureens and pastry bowls can be excellent for flowers. Provided that it holds water, a container need not necessarily be discarded because it has chipped edges or is generally shabby. It is a good idea to get together several practical people and to have a 'vase repairing day'.

Repairing vases does make quite a mess and it is best if it can take place in a barn or outhouse. If this is not possible and it has to be done in a house or a corner of the church, first spread out a large sheet of polythene and then put dust sheets on top of it. Scrub all the vases and let them dry, and where necessary repair chips, cracks, etc, with *Polyfilla*. When this has hardened, rub it down, and paint the container with a matt plastic paint. I find that shades of grey, black and dull green fade into church backgrounds. If the church is whitewashed, then white vases are useful.

If the style of the building is formal, and the decoration includes gold, a vase with its decoration picked out in gilt paint can be very effective: but you need a clever painter and the gilt needs to be used in a sparing way! Some churches, especially modern ones, have walls painted in strong colours; or the colour may be in the windows, curtains or carpets. In such a case a vase can with advantage be painted so as to pick up the colour in the building and flowers can be used to tone in with it.

Containers should always suit the building. Of course, when filled with flowers many are hardly visible, and so can be used in any church. What I hate to see is a simple country church filled with formal gilded or marbled pedestals and containers which in no way suit the background.

It is possible to obtain lovely glass-fibre copies of antique urns; but while they are beautiful, they are also heavy to carry and expensive to buy. To-day they are often replaced by excellent plastic reproductions. It is worthwhile to collect copper and brass preserving pans or copper casseroles, because they look well in most churches and provide a becoming background for flowers. Copper is especially attractive if placed on a wooden chest or table, when it reflects the flowers well. It may be possible to find a local pottery which will make vases to order: I have seen very good wide-topped vases made to order in colours of the church's choice. Large earthenware and copper jugs are excellent for branches of foliage. Silver goblets can enhance a formal church, particularly one of the Regency period, and here gilt and marble can also be used to advantage. If you are using a silver goblet or any other container which might be scratched or otherwise damaged by chicken wire, it is essential to use a lining to protect it.

CONTAINERS FOR USE ON PEDESTALS

Some pedestals have their own containers, but when using a pedestal it is better to have a bowl with a wide top. Good plastic bowls can be bought in black and in white. I prefer, however, to use an ordinary plastic washing-up bowl with a rim over which one can fold the chicken wires. *Fablon*, which is sold by the metre, has a sticky back and adheres well to plastic. With a marbled pattern in black and grey, it can be used to cover the bowl, which is then filled with flowers and fades out of sight. Casseroles, pâté dishes and mixing bowls all sit well on a flat pedestal top.

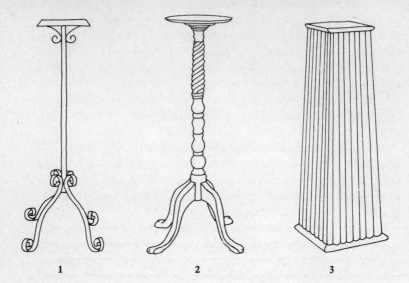

1   2   3

PEDESTALS

Pedestals are used with containers on top to give greater height to
flower arrangements. There are many varieties. One of the most useful
is the wrought iron type, for it fits all periods and types of church (Fig. 1).
Often there will be a local foundry where pedestals can be made to order,
and this is especially useful when a church wants a pair. It is better to
have a pedestal made with a flat top with holes in each corner than to
have a box-like container fixed rigidly to the top. A separate container
of your choice can then be used, and if necessary secured by wire
through the holes. Victorian bedposts (Fig. 2) and wooden plant stands
make excellent pedestals.

Papier mâché pedestals can be made to look like green marble and
gilded, and very effective they are in a church with formal decoration.

There are excellent wooden fluted stands (Fig. 3) which can be
painted any colour and these are suitable for modern churches. Two
of the best pedestals which I have ever seen were two discarded dental
spitoons. They were a reasonable height and the wide basins made perfect containers!

CONSTRUCTIONS

When a church is being decorated for a special occasion it is very helpful to use flowers so as to provide colour from the floor to a given

height. There are various sorts of constructions designed for this purpose. There are three kinds at St Albans Abbey, one in iron and two more simple ones made basically in wood. The method by which they are made is seen from the accompanying drawings.

In the case of the one made of iron a flat base is used onto which is bolted an upright. Containers are affixed to the upright at intervals of about a foot. A seed box for *Oasis* is placed on the flat base (Fig. 4). The wooden constructions are less stable, but very easy for a handyman to make. The structure of the first is similar to the iron one except that flat wooden shelves are fixed up the post at intervals and on them are secured the flat plates which are sold to hold bricks of *Oasis*. Again, a seed box for *Oasis* is placed at the base (Fig. 5). This construction has the advantage of being very simple. The other type of wooden construction has a wooden cross-piece as a base, to which is fixed an upright wooden pole. A hole is made in the middle of a round washing-up bowl, which is dropped down over the top of the pole to form the bottom tier of the construction. Metal hub caps, again with holes in the centre, are fixed to the pole to form the second and third tiers. A cone is lashed to the top of the pole (Fig. 6). The bowl and the hub-caps will be filled with *Oasis* and the cone with water.

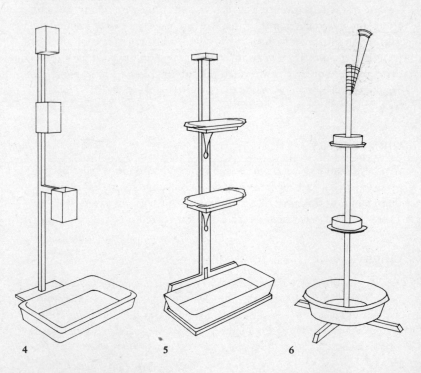

4   5   6

3
Aids to Flower Arranging and Basic Arrangers' Cupboard

Church arrangers need certain basic equipment to help them to arrange flowers and to extend their ideas. This equipment is often spoken of as the 'mechanics' of flower arranging, that term being used to cover any material aid which the arranger employs. The following are all part of the mechanics.

STUB SCISSORS

These, which are available from most flower shops and garden centres, are one of the best inventions. They cut not only wire of any sort but also plant material, from the most delicate variety to large branches of foliage. An instrument which carries out both these operations is worth its weight in gold. They are now almost golden in price, so do watch that they are not swept away with the rubbish! I sew a large piece of tape onto mine, with my name on it, particularly when I am working with other arrangers!

WIRE CUTTERS

Although stub scissors are excellent for small amounts of wire cutting, persistent use in cutting large pieces of chicken wire inevitably makes them blunt, so it is advisable to have a pair of wire cutters as well. There are small, neat ones which most florists sell.

CHICKEN WIRE

To-day there are very many aids to help to anchor your flowers in position, but much the most basic and essential is 2-inch gauge chicken wire which can be cut up into suitably sized pieces to fill your vases. If I am buying chicken wire for a church I buy a large roll. This will last for years and is far more economical than the small pieces which may be bought from an ironmonger or a florist's shop. When you are using chicken wire you must have a piece of exactly the right size. If you use too much, it is almost impossible to get the flowers into place. If, on the other hand, you use too little, the wire will slip and the flowers will topple over, probably scattering water onto a precious polished surface in the process. A vase needs at least three layers of wire inside it and when you are cutting your wire from the roll to fit the vase in question you will probably find that to have the correct amount you will need a piece rather bigger than you at first visualize. In time and with practice you will gauge the right size correctly. Fold the piece of wire at each corner until it is crumpled up into layers and gently push it into the container, taking care not to squeeze it too tightly. When you have finished the container should have wire reaching right down to the bottom and forming a dome right over the top (photographs 2,3,4). If you look into the container from above you will see the holes in the ball of chicken wire. The stems of the flowers and other material will be placed into the holes which should accordingly be fairly evenly spaced. If the layers of wire seem to be too closely jammed together, take the piece of wire out, loosen it a bit, and put it back. If it is still wrong, you may have to cut a piece of it off. On the other hand, you may not have enough wire, in which case push it down into the container, cut another piece and wedge it firmly in, pulling it over the top of the container to form the required dome. At one time I was always cutting further pieces of wire: now I usually get the size right the first time. A container which has a handle at each side, like a tureen or an urn, is very useful as you can put a piece of string through the handles to tie the chicken wire in. When an arrangement is complete the string can be cut away as by that time the flowers will be well balanced. If a rather shallow container is used and the chicken wire seems to be slipping, tie a piece of string right over the top of the wire and underneath the container, and then again cut away the string when the arrangement is complete. Plastic-covered chicken wire should be used if the container is a valuable copper or silver one, to avoid scratching. It is vital to get the mechanics right before you start arranging. It is no good persuading yourself that it will be 'all right in the end', because it will not. I remember an occasion very early in my career as a florist when I was doing the flowers for a huge wedding and working against time. An enormous pedestal arrangement hurtled to the floor because the chicken wire was wrongly arranged. Total panic ensued as my fellow florist and I re-did the arrangement almost as the bride's guests arrived at the door. The verger was rightly furious at the floods of water pouring over his lovely clean church — so be warned!

CONES (known as aquapics in the USA)

To enable you to bring your shorter flowers up to the required height very good metal or plastic elongated cones of various sizes are available. They hold water and can be pushed into chicken wire. If an even taller arrangement is required, cones can be lashed onto long sticks and these fitted into the chicken wire. Do remember to fill the cones and when you are topping up the container to top up the cones as well. I remember going back to a church before a wedding to top up the vases and finding that half the arrangements had died because my junior had failed to fill up the cones. If the arrangement is very big it is sometimes easy to overlook a cone — there may be as many as five — so it is as well to make a note of the number so that none are forgotten.

OASIS

This is a useful substance which holds moisture. It may be bought in large oblong bricks or in smaller drum-shaped pieces, and while dry it can be cut with a knife into the size and shape required. Before use it must be soaked for at least 20 minutes. If after that time there are still bubbles, it is likely that the *Oasis* has not fully absorbed all the water required. I use *Oasis* for a shallow container which will not take chicken wire. I put water in the container and then wedge in the *Oasis*. The container must be kept filled with water as otherwise the *Oasis* will eventually dry out. *Oasis* is invaluable for making garlands: see Chapter 8. If the *Oasis* cannot stand in water, it must be put into a plastic bag, because this will keep it reasonably moist. Hard stems can be pushed through the plastic, but for stems which are soft, holes must be bored into it with an instrument such as a knitting needle.

PIN-HOLDERS

These are round metal bases from which numerous spikes protrude upwards. The pin-holder sits at the bottom of the container and provides an additional anchor for heavy branches.

STUB WIRES

These wires, which come in various lengths and gauges and are sold in bundles by weight, can be used in many ways. In the ordinary way one should avoid wiring fresh flowers but if a stem is very bending, as, for instance, in the case of tulips, a wire pushed up the stem will strengthen it; this procedure should, however, be adopted only very sparingly. The natural bending of flower material makes for an interesting arrangement. If a stem has been fractured, a wire can be put up the stem to secure it. Other uses of stub wires are mentioned in the section on garlands (Chapter 8).

REEL WIRE

Silver reel wire varies in gauge, but it is used sometimes to provide a backing for a leaf (figs. 11 and 12, page 55). There is a strong brown reel wire which is very useful for tying chicken wire into a container and for lashing cones securely into a vase. Reel wire can be bought at ironmongers or through flower clubs, and sometimes commercial florists will sell reel wire and stub wires in small bundles.

In addition to these vital mechanics, there is also other equipment which will be found to be very useful.

DUST SHEETS

It is essential to spread a dust sheet on the floor in front of and round a vase which is going to be arranged. All surplus bits and pieces can then be thrown onto the dust sheet and easily removed.

POLYTHENE SHEETING

It is very helpful to have some large pieces of thick polythene sheeting, which should be used, when working on a good wood-block floor or a valuable carpet, as a protection against damp flowers. The sheeting should be laid with a dust sheet on top of it.

TRUG

This is a useful kind of basket both when carrying flowers about the church and when picking flowers.

STRONG STRING

This is useful in many ways and all churches should keep a ball of it.

ATOMIZER OR FLOWER SPRAY

This is used to spray water onto plant material.

BUCKETS

The most useful buckets are green plastic florists' buckets, which are light and which stack easily inside one another. They come in two sizes.

STRIPPERS

This is a gadget used to strip off thorns and surplus leaves. It looks rather like a pair of sugar tongs. If placed just above the area which you want to strip, and pulled downwards, it will in a flash remove whatever one wants removed.

STONES

Some heavy stones can be very helpful and it is as well to have a collection of them. Plastic containers are splendid but have the disadvantage that, being light, they are not very stable. Accordingly, before I arrange flowers in one I first — before putting in the chicken wire — place one or two heavy stones at the bottom of the container, which will prevent it from overturning.

WATERING CAN WITH LONG SPOUT

A watering can with a specially long spout is essential for topping up vases and in particular for reaching through flower material in order to fill up cones.

ARRANGERS' CUPBOARD

The arrangers' work will be more efficient if an area can be set aside in the church where all their equipment can be stored in safety. Most churches have a corner where a large cupboard or shelves can be made available for the arrangers' sole use. In some large churches it may be convenient to have a cupboard in one place and to keep the pedestals and large containers in another area. In such a case it is helpful to identify as, for example, 'Vestry cupboard' or 'bell tower' each place where equipment is kept, and for items always to be returned to the right place. Otherwise time is wasted while church members trip to and fro to various corners of the building in fruitless searches. I have

walked miles – literally – in large churches and cathedrals vainly
searching for lost scissors or wires only to find them eventually in the
wrong place.

It is helpful for a flower guild to build up a basic arrangers' cupboard and I believe that the following list will provide a useful guide.

Contents of cupboard:

1 A variety of containers suited to the building's needs
2 A pair of pedestals
3 At least two old dust sheets
4 A large sheet of polythene
5 Roll of 2-inch-mesh chicken wire
6 Stub scissors
7 Stub wires
8 Reel wire
9 Secateurs (wire cutters)
10 Dust pan and brush
11 Large watering can
12 Small watering can with long spout to top up cones, etc
13 Six cones
14 Several blocks of *Oasis*. (If space is available, it is more economical
    to buy it by the box. Sometimes a local florist will sell it to you, but
    you may have to buy it from New Covent Garden Market.)
15 Several buckets (preferably the plastic ones referred to above)
16 A kettle for use in conditioning flowers as described in Chapter 6
    (and also for restoring arrangers with 'cuppas'!)
17 A hammer (for use in conditioning)
18 A knife for cutting *Oasis*
19 Two large heavy pin-holders
20 Atomizer (flower spray)

The items listed above should meet the needs of most churches, except
on the occasion of flower festivals, in which case it may be necessary
to borrow from neighbouring churches. There is usually a very happy
spirit when churches help each other out at various times.

4
Provision of Flowers

Many flower guilds will include people who have well stocked gardens or friends who will give generously for the church, so that the provision of flowers for Sunday services is no real problem. There are, however, other churches, particularly in urban areas, which will not be self-sufficient. Then there are cathedrals and large churches which are open every day of the week and are decorated with a number of flower arrangements calling for great quantities of material. In the case of buildings like these it is desirable to work out a plan to provide a weekly supply of flowers and foliage. In this chapter I deal with the various ways in which flowers may be provided.

FLOWER POOL

On occasions such as the great festivals when special flower arrangements are usual it is desirable to have a pool of flowers upon which the decorators can draw. An appeal may usefully be made from the pulpit asking the congregation and their friends to contribute flowers and foliage from their gardens; or the appeal may be made in the parish magazine. It is important to stress that quality is the most important thing, not quantity. So, if 12 people each bring only one beautiful delphinium in perfect condition there will be enough to make up a splendid arrangement. A time should be arranged for the flowers to be brought to the church, and there should be members of the flower guild ready waiting to condition them if necessary and to plunge them in buckets of water. If enough people are asked to help a good pool of flowers and foliage is quickly built up. Quite soon the flower guild gets to know the best sources of good material and can ask directly.

THE COUNTRYSIDE

In hedgerows, verges and elsewhere the countryside abounds with interesting arranger's material. In the chapter on dried flowers I refer to suitable wild material to preserve; but there is also lovely fresh material, like cow parsley and elder which will last if conditioned with the boiling water treatment — (page 39), bracken, hips, old man's beard, catkins and pussy willow. Bluebells will last provided they are massed together and conditioned well. There is lots more to be found if you search for it.

THE VEGETABLE AND HERB GARDEN

This is a great provider. My favourites are the globe artichoke, which has splendid grey leaves; fennel, which provides tall feathery green leaves; carrot which has been sown in the spring and left in the ground until the following summer, by which time it is sprouting white flowers about two feet in height and long lasting in water; parsley which has gone to seed, and rhubarb in flower. Marjoram gives a good yellow foliage for low arrangements. There are many other vegetables which one can use, including cauliflowers and ornamental cabbage leaves. When using cauliflowers cut off some of the outside leaves and wedge the head well down into chicken wire.

INDOOR BULBS

After Christmas the choice of flowers is very limited and it is therefore helpful if there are people who are prepared to grow bowls of spring flowers. Obviously this is something which has to be planned in the previous August when the catalogues appear. All the bulbs will be purchased with flower fund money.

If hyacinths are to flower in January it is necessary to buy bulbs specially treated for indoor growing, to plant them in September, and to keep them in the dark for six weeks. They can then be brought into the church even if there is no regular heat. The congregation enjoys watching them develop. When choosing colours it is best to have bulbs all the same colour in each bowl.

Daffodils which are recommended for indoor culture make a welcome splash of colour, as do early double tulips. The latter provide a glorious mixture of bright colours. They develop slowly and faintly resemble double paeonies. If the church is dark the flowers tend to grow taller, so they should be staked.

If the church possesses large urns, soup tureens or preserving pans, which are very good for the display of bulbs, it is a good idea to try to find less valuable containers which will fit inside. The bulbs can be grown in these containers, which, when the bulbs are ready for display, can be dropped inside the urns. Unless inner containers are used, the church will be deprived of its good ones for a long period.

Forced bulbs cannot be used indoors a second time, so when they have finished flowering they should be planted out in the churchyard or in gardens.

GROWING FOR THE CHURCH

There may be space in the churchyard which could be cultivated with shrubs or flowers to provide some material for use by the flower guild. If this is impossible, a local resident might allow a part of his garden to be used for this purpose. Sometimes there is a pensioner who has moved to a flat and misses his own garden who would be happy to help with a project for growing flowers for the church. I know a marvellous old lady who not only cleans the gravestones but also gardens for the church because, she says, 'The young are far too busy and I have little else to do!' So it is worth enquiring. Once you know how much enthusiasm there is you can plan accordingly. How much is grown depends, of course, not only on available volunteers but also on the type of soil and siting of the garden. I am therefore not attempting to give any detailed gardening advice, but I suggest that any of the following would be useful to a busy flower guild, and that climbers should be included for pillar arrangements.

Shrubs and foliage plants

C = climber
E = evergreen
G = suitable for preserving in glycerine
L = Long-lasting in water
P = perennial
S = shrub

Arum italicum marmoratum: beautiful leaf with cream markings.
Bergenia cordifolia purpurea (elephant-leaved saxifrage): **P**; large round leaves **G**
Camellia japonica: **E S**; dark glossy green leaves **L**; also beautiful pink, red and white flowers.
Choisya ternata (Mexican orange): **E S**; glossy green leaves; white flowers.
Cotoneaster: **S**; red berries in autumn.
Cynara scolymus (cardoon): superb green leaves for large groups.
Eleagnus pungens variegata: **E S**; strongly marked yellow bordered leaves **L**

Escallonia: E S; useful curving branches, dark green leaves G.

Garrya elliptica: E S; hardy evergreen catkins (January-March).

Hedera (ivy): C S

    H. canariensis, silvery grey.

    H. colchica dentata variegata, yellow/green.

    H. helix, buttercup yellow.

Helleborus corsicus: E P; large creamy green trusses; needs careful conditioning G.

Hosta (funkia):

    H. albo-marginata, green leaves with white border.

    H. fortunei-albo-picta, in spring, bright yellow edged with pale green.

    H. sieboldiana elegans (H. glauca), blue green.

Hypericum (St John's wort): S gold single flowers.

Ligustrum ovalifolium aureo-marginatum (golden privet): E S; superb golden and green foliage for both tall and small arrangements.

Lonicera (honeysuckle): C S

Philadelphus (mock orange): S; white/cream flowers, avalanche of delicate curved sprays.

    Single. Beauclerk, 6-8 feet.

    Double: Virginal, 8-10 feet.

Polygonatum multiflorum (Solomon's seal).

Pyracantha atalantioides: S; orange berries in autumn; good for harvest festivals.

Senecio greyi: E S; silver grey leaves with almost white backs; easily propagated from cuttings; arrange to show both sides of foliage.

Skimmia japonica: E S; dark green leaves L.

Symphoricarpos albus laevigatus (snowberry): S; white berries in autumn; superb curving stems for all arrangements.

Syringa (lilac): S

    S. sweginzowii, grows up to 12 feet, fragrance of flowers distinguishes it from other lilacs.

    S. vulgaris, double and single white, cream, mauve, pink to dark purple.

Veronica pectinata: E S; slow growing, dark green leaves, thrives in shade L.

Viburnum tinus (laurustinus): S; winter flowering, pale pink flowers, dark foliage.

Viburnum opulus (guelder rose): S; useful white flowers.

Vinca major elegantissima (periwinkle); E S; useful variegated white/green trailing foliage, which lasts well only if conditioned.

Roses

There are endless varieties of roses. The following are a few of those which I have found particularly useful in churches.

Climbers

These look well if they are trained over a church wall and they provide long bending stems which are superb in pedestal and other arrangements. Church flower arrangers should not only use roses singly, but should include long trails which will last provided that they are well conditioned.

'New Dawn' is a perpetual flowering climber which flowers in profusion throughout the summer. It has lovely pale shell pink flowers. Height 10-12 feet.

'Zépherine Drouhin' is a Bourbon variety, strong and hardy with good deep pink flowers. The leaves seem to be prone to spot, so I often remove some of the foliage when arranging in water. It is thornless, which makes it very popular for flower arranging; lasts only if well conditioned.

'Golden Showers': a useful golden-yellow semi-double rose; it flowers freely at intervals; height 7-8 feet.

Floribundas

'Queen Elizabeth': pink, one of the easiest roses to grow and very prolific, splendid if grown as a hedge, when it will reach up to 6 feet, or as a bush; it will provide a continuous supply of beautifully shaped buds and flowers of a good pink which mixes well with all flowers.

'Iceberg': white, tinged with pink; an excellent rose, perfect for flower arranging as the stems bend conveniently and the buds open well at all stages.

'Dearest': salmon pink; it makes an effective bed; it is free-flowering and lasts very well in water.

Hybrid Teas

When I started as a florist 35 years ago the best pink roses for commercial use were 'Madame Butterfly', 'Lady Sylvia' and 'Ophelia'. They travelled and lasted well. They then disappeared from florists' shops, but fortunately bushes are available in some nurseries. If they can be found, they are superb for the flower arranger and for the gardener.

'Peace': a superb rose for churches, deep yellow stained with cerise
pink, opening up into large flowers; it is best if kept as a shrub and
lightly pruned.

'Grandpa Dickson': lemon yellow fading to cream; huge heads; excellent in large pedestal arrangements.

'Pascali': white; opens into a beautifully shaped flower; perfect for weddings and christenings, it grows well in cold areas.

Dahlias

If there is space available it is worthwhile to give it over to a bed of dahlias. They are useful, flowering into late September and early October.
There is an enormous choice. If there is a good dahlia nursery locally,
look at the plants in flower and choose some with large heads, which
are good in pedestal arrangements, and some of the cactus variety,
which have pretty star-shaped flowers with pointed petals, and the
smaller pom-pom. This mixture will give good varied large and small
shapes for the church's use.

Biennials, perennials and annuals

There are so many flowers which grow easily and are excellent for
church flower arrangers that it is very hard to pick out particular types.
Here are listed varieties which have proved easy to grow and at the same
time invaluable, but no doubt the list can be added to year after year. If
there is very little interest in growing plants and there is an empty bed,
why not grow *alchemilla* and some *euphorbia*?

A = annual
B = biennial
H A = hardy annual
H H A = half hardy annual
P = perennial

Achillea (yarrow): **P**; yellow; dries; July-September.
Alchemilla major (mollis) (lady's mantle): **P**; lime green flowers; dries;
April-June.
Antirrhinum majus (snapdragon): **P**; mixed colours; July-September.
Aquilegia (columbine): **P**; mixed colours; April-June.
Aster novi-belgi (Michaelmas daisy): **P**; late flowering.
Arctic, double white.
Elizabeth Bright, double pink.

Campanula (Canterbury bells) white and purple; June-August.
Chrysanthemum maximum (shasta daisy): P; July.
    Esther Read, double white.
    Phyllis Smith, single white.
Delphinium: A; white, mauve, blue; seed heads and flowers dry; June.
Delphinium ajacia (larkspur): H H A; pink, white, blue; dries, June.
Dianthus barbatus (sweet william): B; mixed reds, white, purple;
    dries; May-June.
Euphorbia: P
    E. robbiae (spurge), dark green leaves, pale green bracts in spring;
    long-lasting if conditioned well.
    E. wulfeni (giant spurge); large heads particularly suitable for pede-
    stal arrangements.
Nicotiana alata (tobacco plant): H H A; greenish white; also hybrid
    species, pink, red and crimson; July-September.
Paeonia (paeony): P
    P. lacriflora (single)
        Emma, carmine pink.
        Jan Van Leenven, large white, gold centre.
        Pink Delight, rose pink, gold stamens.
    P. officinalis (double), red, pink, white; superb foliage which goes
    gold and red in autumn.
Phlox: P; July-September
    Charles Curtis, cherry red.
    Evangeline, rose pink.
    Mia Ruys and Rembrandt, white.
Rudbeckia hirta (black-eyed Susan): P; yellow, golden yellow brown
    centre; July-September.
Sedum: P; September-October
    S. atropurpureum, pale pink flowers, superb copper foliage.
    S. spectabile, bright pink flowers; dries.

Bulbs, corms, etc

If you have decided to make a flower bed in the churchyard, you
could include spring flowers like daffodils and narcissus, or daffodils
could be planted under trees. If you have a special cutting bed in a
garden, include a row of white or pink hyacinths, as well as daffodils
and tulips. I find the 'lily flowering' variety of tulip, with graceful
pointed petals, particularly pretty and useful in May when the earlier
spring flowers have finished.

    Gladiolus (corms) grow well in a sunny position and well drained bed. If the planting of them is staggered over several weeks they will provide flowers from May to September. They need to be weeded and staked, and to be lifted in November, so they do entail quite a lot of work.

The nerine *bowdenii* is quite one of the most valuable of bulbs. Many people say that nerines need a south wall, but they grow well in beds among shrubs provided that they get enough light and sun. They are sometimes slow to flower, but once they have blossomed they increase every year. They last at least a fortnight if picked as they are just coming out.

5
Dried Material

During the winter months when gardens are bare and flowers are very expensive to buy, dried plant material is invaluable to the church florist. In the past the methods of preservation were limited and the winter colour range was confined to shades of brown and beige. Nowadays there are several methods in use which allow the natural colours to be kept, so that it is possible to have beautiful arrangements with wide ranges of shades as well as interesting textures. However, the vase should from time to time be re-arranged. I saw a vase once which had remained in a church for three years untouched and gathering clouds of dust! Eventually it seemed to be part of the building! If you amass a good collection of dried material you can ring the changes with it, or mix it with fresh foliage or flowers.

There are some excellent specialized books on plant preservation, so this chapter is concerned with only those methods which are the easiest for a busy flower guild. Drying does, however, take time, and it is important to take trouble: otherwise you will end up with very tatty bits and pieces!

DRYING BY HANGING

This method is not as sinister as it sounds! Some seed heads, grasses and flowers dry tied in bunches and hung upside down.

When you are planning a dried collection, keep an eagle eye on your flower border. When the seed heads have formed cut them before they are spotted or spoilt by damp. If flowers are to be preserved they must be in perfect condition. By the time they start to drop or wilt it is too late to use them.

In the autumn go to the country and you will find the hedgerows full of seed heads. Again pick only the perfect ones and only the amount with which you can cope: otherwise you stuff your car with material which inevitably sheds seeds everywhere, and this is not popular!

When you are ready to dry your material gather about six stems and tie them so that the heads are not bunched together. The air must

1   Mixed foliage and green hellebores with 'Enchantment' lilies

2 'Construction' at St John the Baptist, Great Gaddesden. This was one of a pair leading to the chancel

3   Flowers and vegetables arranged for harvest festival

4   St Mary Magdalene, Whipsnade. Christmas wall plaque and garland made with holly, looped red ribbon and spray carnations

5   St Mary Magdalene, Whipsnade. White and green material including carefully
conditioned weeping willow in a brown china jug

circulate freely. Tie a piece of string from a nail in one wall to a nail in the opposite wall. Hang the bunches from the string well spaced out from one another. They will drop a number of seeds, so spread a dust-sheet under the hanging area. The first time I tried this method it failed because the room, in a very old house, was not absolutely dry. The next time I kept a night storage heater on at a medium setting and the bunches dried in about three weeks. A garage or shed is only suit-able if quite dry. If you are fortunate enough to have a very warm place like a kitchen or laundry with sufficient space, the material will dry much more quickly: and the quicker the better. Do remember that long stems and large seed heads are heavy when you start to dry them, so the string must be firmly tied and made taut.

When you are quite sure that the material is dry — it should be papery and dry to the touch — give it a last shake, untie the bunches, and then store it in long boxes in layers of tissue paper. It is fragile when dried so careful storing is important. Churches need long stems of dried material and if suitable boxes are difficult to come by there are some plants like honesty and achillea which can safely be put to stand in a corner of the building in empty jugs or buckets.

The following can be successfully preserved by the hanging method:

Acanthus: white and mauve flowers; pick when flowers are in good condition; useful for large groups as they give height.

Achillea (yarrow): yellow flower heads; also dry by upright method.

Alchemilla major (mollis) (lady's mantle): lime green flowers. Both flowers and the tiny leaves will dry.

Allium cepa (onion): dry large round seed heads.

Althaea (hollyhock): Seed heads.

Bulrush: Brown spikes; pick when the brown spikes are half devel-oped.

Carrot leaves: pale green.

Clarkia: pink and purple flowers.

Clematis vitalba (old man's beard): pick before the heads are too fluffy. Strip off leaves. If preserved in glycerine leave the leaves on as they go an interesting brown.

Conium maculatum (hemlock): orangey brown.

Cynara scolymus (globe artichoke): large purple heads; heads change to cream after drying.

Delphinium: pink, mauve, blue and white flowers. Dry both seed heads and flowers. To preserve the flowers pick when some buds are still unopened.

Delphinium ajacis (larkspur): pink, mauve and white flowers.

Digitalis (foxglove): preserve seed heads.

Dipsacus fullonum (teasel): useful seed heads.

Dock: lime green to dark red; also dries well in glycerine.

Echinops ritro (globe thistle): grey blue colour. Very prickly stems so wear gloves to prepare!

Grasses.

Helichrysum bracteatum (everlasting flower): mixed. Push a stub of wire up the stem to the base of the flower head before drying: otherwise it flops.

Lunaria annua (honesty): purple and white flowers. Cut when the seed heads are bone dry, shake well and remove outer covering leaving translucent silvery seed pods.

Lupinus (lupin): mixed colours. Dry seed heads. Pick straight and bending stems.

Molucella laevis (bells of Ireland): lime green flowers. Dry to pale parchment colour. Also dry well in glycerine.

Papaver (poppy): pink and reds. Collect all seed heads, from tiny wild ones to large cultivated varieties.

Physalis franchettii (Chinese lanterns or Cape gooseberry): dry the seed heads. Cut when some of the calyces have not yet ripened.

Solidago (golden rod): golden flower spikes; can dry upright.

DRYING IN WATER

Some flowers dry well if left standing in water in an upright container like a tall jug or a florist's bucket until dry. Hydrangeas are best preserved in water. Pick them when the heads are just starting to dry at the edges, and put them in water which reaches half way up their stems. Most people agree that in every collection of hydrangeas there are one or two which for no apparent reason die rather then dry!

UPRIGHT DRYING

This method is used if space is short. Simply place the stems in an empty tall jug or florist's bucket and let them dry off in a place where they must be dry and should preferably be warm. The buckets can easily overturn, so put a brick or stone in the bottom.

The following can be successfully preserved by upright drying:

Achillea (yarrow); yellow flower heads.

Cynara scolymus (globe artichoke); pick when purple flower heads are half developed. Strip off prickles and leaves.

Dianthus barbatus (sweet william); useful mauve and pink flowers. Pick when flowers are not fully open.

DRYING BY PRESSING

The best way to press and dry leaves is to lift up a bit of carpet, put down several layers of newspaper, and onto this place the leaves, making sure that they are quite flat. If they crease or bend they will be useless. Make sure too that the leaves do not touch. Cover them with two more layers of newspaper and put back the carpet. The more they are walked on the better! There are differences of opinion as to how long it takes for the leaves to dry out completely. I find that at least three weeks are needed and very often longer. I once forgot about a collection and did not find them until a year later when spring cleaning. They were super!

I have become very keen on drying leaves in this way, both for my house and church. It is a good way of having different coloured leaves to mix with flowers in the winter and with those few early spring flowers. The dried leaves are of course very brittle indeed. It is helpful to wire some of them with reel or fuse wire onto firm twigs (see Chapter 8).

The following leaves can be dried in this way:

Beech: pick the branches in various stages of colour and be sure that they are quite flat.

Bracken: choose different colours from green to red.

Ferns: both large and small dry excellently. When I stay in Scotland in a friend's house I dry ferns at the beginning of the holiday and they are fine in just about a fortnight when we leave; empty dress boxes always travel with me!

Hosta.

DRYING IN GLYCERINE OR ANTI-FREEZE

A solution of glycerine or the anti-freeze mixture used in the radiator of a car is an excellent method of preserving foliage and berries. Material preserved in this way keeps its natural sheen and does not become brittle or dry as does material dried by the other methods. The disadvantage is that the material changes colour, becoming much darker. I suggest that in the case of a small flower guild with little time or space to give to preservation this is the most practical method. There is some cost involved, but if the material is stored carefully when not in use it should last for years.

Take the material which is to be preserved and strip off all bottom leaves. Split the stems. The ends of hard-wooded stems should be hammered. The point of splitting the stems is to make sure that the solution reaches upwards into every part of the plant.

Place the preserving mixture in a narrow container: earthenware jugs or jars are excellent. Ensure that the liquid reaches 2 inches up the stems. Keep an eye on the material as some stems drink more quickly than others and may absorb all the liquid before preservation is complete. If this happens, top up with more of the mixture. Leaves are ready when they have quite changed colour and there is no sign of brittleness. If there is some of the solution left, store it in an air-tight jar and it can be used again.

Do experiment with different foliages. I have found beech, escallonia, helleborus, corsicus, laurel, mahonia and rhododendron particularly good, although they do change to a very dark green or brown. Most berries preserve well in this way. Spraying them afterwards with an ordinary hair lacquer helps to preserve them.

The glycerine solution consists of one part of glycerine to two parts of very hot water. As a container I use a large 'instant' coffee jar with a lid, as the solution needs to be shaken well: otherwise the glycerine will drop to the bottom. If hard-wooded stems are to be preserved the glycerine should be boiled first.

The anti-freeze solution consists of one part of anti-freeze to one part of water.

IRONING

This is an effective and quick method for preserving single leaves. Place the leaves between layers of blotting paper and iron with a warm iron until they are dry.

The following leaves iron well:

Horse-chestnut
Iris pseudacorus variegatus
Maple

DRYING IN DESSICANTS

The other methods described are more practical for a busy church flower guild. If, however, you are anxious to experiment with silica gel, write to the American Museum in Bath which sells an excellent little pamphlet describing this method of preservation.

A good collection of dried material is a great stand-by: but do remember that if a church wants to keep it in good condition it must when not in use be carefully packed in tissue paper in strong boxes. Market boxes in which flowers have travelled are perfect for this purpose. They must be stored away in a dry place. Do not overfill the box as brittle leaves split easily.

6
Conditioning

In the flower world 'conditioning' means preparing flowers and foliage well in advance of use to ensure that they will last as long as possible. If you are short of time because you have a heavy schedule over a short period it is far better to pick or buy flowers well in advance and if necessary to give them 48 hours in water than to leave everything until the last day. Flowers and foliage will last better given a long drink in a cool area than with a short drink, possibly in a warm place. I have proved this many times — I may say in the teeth of opposition!

BASIC CUTTING INSTRUCTIONS

When you are cutting from the garden or hedgerows do not hack or pull, but cut firmly with stub scissors or secateurs. If you have planned your arrangement in advance, you will know roughly how many stems of each colour and variety you will need. It is useful to observe the habit of growth of the flowers, and to pick some bending to the right and others bending to the left, together with a proportion of good straight stems.

If possible, pick in the evening, when it is cool and the flowers can drink for 12 hours at least, which is good for them. If for some reason you are forced to pick in warm sunlight, take with you buckets half-filled and put the flowers straight into water as you go round the garden. If you are out in the country and you have an estate car or a car with a large boot, have buckets of water with you and then, provided that the stems are not too long, the material which you pick can travel in them. I put string round the buckets and tie them to something in the car to stop them from falling over. Always take off all leaves which would be below the water line. If the material is too tall for buckets, wrap it in damp newspapers.

When you have picked and collected together all the material which you need, there are various forms of treatment which you can use to make it last.

WATER

With one or two exceptions flowers and foliage last better if placed in buckets of warm water. If, on the other hand, roses are coming out too quickly, wrap about six stems together in newspaper and plunge them in cold water with ice blocks. This will stop them from opening too soon.

HAMMERING

All hard-wooded stems should be placed on a hard surface and the ends should be hammered to split them. This will ensure that water reaches the tops of the stems. The lower leaves should be taken off before plunging the stems into deep warm water.

BOILING WATER TREATMENT

Put the flowers in a bucket and pour in boiling water so that it comes about an inch up the stems. Count to about ten, and then fill up the container with cold water. This treatment is essential for poppies, delphiniums and euphorbia, but in fact most flowers can be conditioned in this way. The reason? The treatment prevents cells from being blocked and allows sap lost in the water to get up the stems.

SEARING

This is an alternative to the boiling-water method, and provides a quick way of sealing ends of flowers. Euphorbia, for instance, bleeds off a sticky substance, and searing will prevent this bleeding. Simply hold the end of the stem over a lighted candle or match.

STARCH

Some leaves and ferns need strengthening. This can be effected by putting them in a solution of two teaspoonfuls of starch to one-and-a-half pints of water. This process, by stiffening them, will make them easier to arrange.

FLOATING

If you have a large basin or baby bath full of water and simply float in it the leaves of such flowers as hostas and arums, limp ones will revive very quickly. This treatment is invaluable for hellebores.

FILLING HOLLOW STEMS WITH WATER

An alternative to boiling stems is to fill hollow ones with water and then plug the ends with cotton wool.

SPRAYING

Most florists' shops sell a fine water spray. When your arrangement is complete, spray both flowers and foliage with water, especially in hot weather, when they need this added moisture. Indeed, if it is really hot, spray twice a day. If your arrangement is up against a wall painting or valuable panelling, or anything else which water might damage, make sure that you get a friend to hold up a tea towel behind the vase as a protection to the background.

SUGAR

Sugar puts back a needed substance into tulips. If they are wilting, take them out of their container, cut the stems about half-an-inch from the bottom, and refill the container with warm water, adding about a dessertspoonful of sugar for every two pints of water.

PRICKING STEMS

The stems of some flowers form bubbles, thereby preventing water from reaching the blossom. Tulips and hellebores are particularly prone to this. The treatment is to take the stem and to pierce it just below the head very carefully with a needle, continuing the pricking down the stem at intervals of one inch. This will ensure that water reaches the blossom.

SNIPPING ENDS

Unless you are using the hammering method described above, always cut each stem upwards for about half-an-inch from the end before putting it into water. If you later rearrange the vase, take each stem out and snip it again in the same way.

FILLING THE VASE

When you have completed the arrangement, fill the container to as near the top as you dare! In about two hours' time, refill. It is in the first two hours that flowers drink most. If the vase is on a polished table, it is wise to stand it on a cloth when you first fill it, in case you overfill or the flowers siphon. Leave the cloth for a bit, but do remember to remove it later!

TREATMENT FOR SHOP-BOUGHT FLOWERS

If you buy flowers at a shop and do not know the florist well, it is as well to condition all flowers when you get home or to the church. The very best florist may have a junior who has a lapse and skips the conditioning which she has been taught to do.

CHRYSAL

This is a substance which is put into water to make flowers last, and it certainly does help enormously. I have used it for press shows when flowers have been put on display after coming straight from the airport, with no chance of normal conditioning: but it is expensive.

RETAINING ROOTS

Some flowers, for example, poinsettias, bleed when cut and therefore do not last well. If, however, they are taken out of a pot roots and all, and carefully put into a polythene bag tied at the top of the root, they can be used in flower decorating. This is a good way of using any kind of potted plant material, such as *Begonia rex*, ivy, chlorophytum, etc, mixed with cut flowers. When the flowers are dead the plants can be re-potted. When flowers are needed at a height, they can be lashed to the tops of sticks.

DISASTERS

If several flowers in an arrangement wilt, take them out; in most cases the boiling water treatment (see above) will revive them. Put them in a bucket and give them a further drink for an hour or so. Then place them back in the arrangement.

If heads of roses droop, take them out, cut them a little shorter, slice them up the stem for half an inch, and plunge them into warm water for an hour or two.

If hellebores wilt, take them out, cut their ends, and float them in water for an hour. They are best used in low bowls with their stems not too long.

If tulips wilt, take them out and recondition by putting them in a bucket of deep water with sugar (see above).

TREATMENT OF PARTICULAR FLOWERS AND FOLIAGE

I am sure that I am considered by churches and flower classes to be a 'conditioning' bore because I am always, as my children say, 'nagging on' about it: but I must stress that it is useless taking time and thought in arranging beautiful vases in your church if the material is not properly conditioned, for it will not last and heartache and irritation will be caused to all concerned. It really is important to allow enough time for the conditioning process.

There follows a list of flowers and of foliage of trees and shrubs which I find most useful in church flower arranging and some of which needs to be specially conditioned or preserved. If it is to last, material should have stems cut or hammered as the case may be (see above) and be given a long drink of water before being arranged. I have not in the following list referred to these steps in the conditioning process: I assume that they will always be taken. In this list I have generally followed my usual practice of giving the botanical name with the popular name, if there is one, in brackets: trees and some plants, on the other hand, will be much better known to the reader by their common names, so I have given these alone. Many lesser known flowers are omitted: the list is intended as a guide to only the more usual material. *Denotes material which lasts well and ** material which lasts particularly well.

Achillea (yarrow)**

Agapanthus*: give long warm drink.

Alchemilla major (mollis)*: boiling water treatment, then long drink.

Alder*: give long warm drink. If picked in January and put into warm water in a warm atmosphere the catkins will develop.

Amaranthus (love lies bleeding)*: take off the leaves as they easily wilt.

Amaryllis*: give long warm drink.

Anemone: Give very long warm drink. If necks become limp, cut stems a second time and give another long drink in cold water.

Angelica: Boiling water treatment: then long drink in cold water.

Anthriscus sylvestris (cow parsley)*: boiling water treatment: very long drink.

Antirrhinum (snapdragon): the forced variety needs boiling water treatment and long drink.

Aquilegia (columbine)**: warm water for two or three hours. If dead flowers are removed, new ones will open.

*Artemisia**

Arum leaves** (*calla* leaves in USA): float for about an hour. If it is desired to give them a shiny appearance and to make them last longer, float them for 24 hours in a weak solution of starch.

Arum lilies** (*calla* lilies in USA): give long drink with water right up to the flower heads.

*Aster** (Michaelmas daisy; China aster in USA): remove foliage before giving long drink.

Azalea: give long warm drink.

Beech: give long warm drink.

Berries: give long warm drink.

*Buddleia**: boiling water treatment: then long drink.

Bulrush*: pick when in good condition (before splitting). To stop splitting, spray with hair lacquer.

Calendula (marigold).

Camellia: the foliage is wonderfully long lasting: I have had it over three weeks. Put in warm water. Care should be taken not to touch the flowers as they bruise easily.

Campanula (Canterbury bell)*: give long warm drink. Remove any dead heads as they appear.

Chamaenerion augustifolium (willow herb: *epilobium* in USA): the flower does not last well but is helped by being put into boiling water. When going to seed and slightly fluffy, it is an excellent addition to autumn arrangements, but do not cut when too fluffy as the fluff spreads everywhere.

Cheiranthus (wallflower): give long warm drink. Try to arrange in deepish water.

Cherry: give warm drink for at least six hours, preferably longer.

Choisya ternata (Mexican orange)*

*Chrysanthemum***

*Clarkia***: boiling water treatment: then long drink.

Clematis vitalba (old man's beard)**: boiling water treatment: then long drink. Strip off some of the leaves.

Convallaria majalis (lily of the valley): the outdoor varieties do generally reasonably well. The cloche and forced varieties do not last at all well. Give long warm drink.

*Cotoneaster***

Cynara cardunculus (cardoon)*

Cynara scolymus (globe artichoke)*: cut when the leaves have been on the plant for some weeks. Boiling water treatment: then submerge in a bath of cold water for several hours.

Cytisus (broom): foliage on its own lasts well and needs no special treatment. When in flower, the ends should be put in very hot water.

Daffodil: see *narcissus*.

Dahlia: put ends of stems in boiling water: then give long drink.

Daphne: boiling water treatment: then long drink in cold water.

Delphinium: put ends of stems in boiling water; or fill ends with water and plug with cotton wool.

Delphinium ajacis (larkspur): give long warm drink.

Dianthus (carnation)*: break the stems, if possible at the joints; if not, at the ends. Give long warm drink.

Dianthus barbatus (sweet william)**: give long warm drink.

Digitalis (foxglove): put in warm water for a good six hours.

Endymion nonscriptus (bluebell or wild hyacinth: not in USA): remove white ends. Use massed in deep water. Some will last well, but most of them for only a few days and some for only a few hours. (This is not the same as *campanula rotundifolia*, the harebell or Scottish bluebell).

*Escallonia***: boiling water treatment.

*Eucalyptus**

Euphorbia (spurge)*: boiling water treatment: then long drink.

Forsythia: put in warm water for several hours. To force blossoms, put sprays in warm water in the kitchen or airing cupboard. Depending upon the amount of heat, the flowers take about a month or more to open.

Fuchsia: boiling water treatment: then long drink.

*Garrya elliptica**: can be forced in a warm place.

*Geranium**: boiling water treatment: then long drink.

Gerbera (Barberton daisy): boiling water treatment: then long warm drink. If the stems seem limp at the flower head, wrap the stems in paper while the flowers are drinking. The lasting time varies, but sometimes they last well.

*Gladiolus***: Pick while still in bud. If you want to hold them back for a special occasion, put them out of water on a stone floor or in a box with a lid. I have known them to open beautifully after a fortnight of this bold treatment. Then cut the ends and give long warm drink.

*Godetia**: remove lower foliage. Give long warm drink.

Hedera (ivy)**: put in warm water.

Helleborus: all hellebores need their stems pricked at intervals from bellow the flower to below the water line. The green variety needs boiling water treatment and the flowers need to be in water up to their heads overnight. If they flag after arranging, take them out, cut the ends, and float them for an hour. All hellebores are better arranged in groups in deep water: then they will last reasonably well. If in shallow water, they quickly flag.

Holly: this lasts best if arranged in *Oasis*. If it has to be cut in advance, leave it on the lawn, but protect it from the birds.

Hosta (funkia)*: float leaves for two to three hours.

Hydrangea: boiling water treatment. Submerge whole head and stem under water for a few hours. Needs to be sprayed often as it absorbs moisture through the flower heads.

Hypericum (rose of Sharon or St John's wort)*: cut stems at a slant.

Iris: cut the stems and put in cold water: one of the exceptions to the 'warm water' rule.

Jasminum nudiflorum (winter flowering jasmine)*: boiling water treatment: then long drink.

Kale*: decorative kale and cabbage is excellent for church arrangements. Pare ends of stems to a tapering point. Make criss-crosses up stem, one way and then the other, and put into cold water.

Lathyrus odoratus (sweet pea): arrange in shallow water.

Ligustrum (golden privet)**

Lilium (lily)**: all varieties (e.g. longiflorum, the Easter lily) are long lasting and excellent for church arrangements. Cut the stems at a slant and give long drink in cold water.

Lime*: strip off the leaves, leaving the pale lime-green flowers and bracts.

Lonicera (honeysuckle): put in hot water.

Lupinus (lupin): put the ends in boiling water, wrap them in newspaper, and give long warm drink. Keeping them wrapped will help to keep them stiff.

Magnolia grandiflora : pick in bud. Give long drink in very hot water. Leave for several hours.

*Mahonia bealci**

Maple: young branches should be submerged under water for some hours.

Matthiola (stock): give long warm drink.

Acacia dealbata (mimosa): Give warm drink and spray twice a day. If buying in large quantities and it is in a cardboard pack, leave it unopened until you are ready to use it. I have kept it for 48 hours in this way. It is now sold treated with a preservative which helps it to last.

Molucella laevis (bells of Ireland)*: remove all leaves. Cut stems at a slant. Give long drink.

Narcissus: prefers shallow water.

Nerine bowdenii**

Nicotiana alata (tobacco plant)**: give long warm drink.

Paeonia (paeony): if for immediate use, hammer ends well and give long warm drink. If you want to hold them back for a special occasion, pick and place on stone floor for three or four days. When wanted, hammer ends and give long warm drink.

Papaver (poppy): Cut when colour is just beginning to show and put ends in boiling water. If the stems are then re-cut, put into boiling water again.

Philadelphus (mock orange): remove most of the foliage. Put in warm water.

Phlox: put stems in boiling water. Then give long drink in warm water.

Poinsettia: better with the roots and some soil left on and tied into polythene bag: otherwise it bleeds. If only used for a short time, it can be re-potted.

Polyanthus (primrose in USA): give long warm drink. They last better if kept massed on shortish stems.

Prunus laurocerasus (laurel)**: give long warm drink.

Pyracantha atalantioides

Pyrethrum: give long warm drink.

Rhododendron: give long warm drink. If it seems to be wilting at all, put the stems in boiling water and then give them long drink.

Rosa (rose): slice the ends for about half an inch up the stems. Give long warm drink. They are better arranged in fairly deep water. If you have forced flowers out of season and the heads start to droop before they have opened, cut the stems fairly short and give long warm drink. If in hot weather you want to prevent the buds from opening too quckly, wrap them, and place them in water with blocks of ice until required.

Rudbeckia: boiling water treatment: then long drink in warm water.

Senecio greyi.

Skimmia japonica**

Solidago (golden rod)*

Sorbus (rowan or mountain ash, white beam)*

Symphoricarpos albus laevigatus (snowberry): give long warm drink.

Syringa (lilac)*: remove nearly all the leaves; if they are left on the branch the flowers do not last well. If you want the natural foliage, use it separately. Forced: the longer the stems, the less time the flowers last.

Tulipa (tulip): cut off the white ends: Give long warm drink. If you wish to keep some straight, wrap heads in newspaper. In a large mixed vase it is better to let some find their own shape and to have some wrapped before you arrange them. If they are at all limp, they will perk up if sugar is put in the water, about a dessertspoonful to an average vase.

Viburnum tinus (laurustinus)*

Viburnum opulus (guelder rose: snowball in USA): give long warm drink.

Vinca major elegantissima (periwinkle): boiling water treatment: then long drink. Only suitable for foliage.

Zinnia: put the ends in boiling water. In the case of large-headed varieties a wire can be pushed down the middle of the flower into the stem to prevent the stem bending with the weight of the head. The big flowers do not last particularly well.

7
First Steps

Many people who arrange lovely flowers in their own houses are terrified if it is suggested to them that they help in a flower guild or take part in a flower festival. I used to teach at further education classes and invariably when I suggested that it would be nice if the pupils extended their field and helped their local church there were cries of 'Goodness, no! We could not possibly do anything so grand!': or, another favourite, 'We would not know where to start!' The purpose of this chapter is to show the new church flower arranger how to start and what to consider step by step.

The most important point is to realize why we want flowers in churches. One reason is that flowers give an added dimension to the building. They provide a way of expressing our gratitude for all that the Church stands for. Furthermore, flowers can be used to accentuate certain architectural features. For instance, if there is a beautiful ceiling, flower balls hung at a height make the visitor look up. Attention can be drawn to beautiful carvings by placing a flower arrangement nearby.

There may be another, quite different, reason. The building may be hideous. Alas! some are. In that case huge bowls of flowers can be used to hide the worst features. So before you make any plan decide what your flowers are to do. Are they to enhance or to hide? If they are to enhance, make sure that you do not get so carried away that you end by hiding!

BACKGROUND

To decide what is the purpose of your particular arrangement go to the church and look at the background. When I am working in a church which I do not know I spend time walking round the whole building and soaking up the atmosphere and character. Then when I know the exact area which my flowers will decorate I sit down and study it from all angles. In the case of a cathedral or large church with great soaring arches the flower material will have to be sufficiently substantial and important to balance these features, and the arrangement must include flowers which will be visible from a distance. A small country

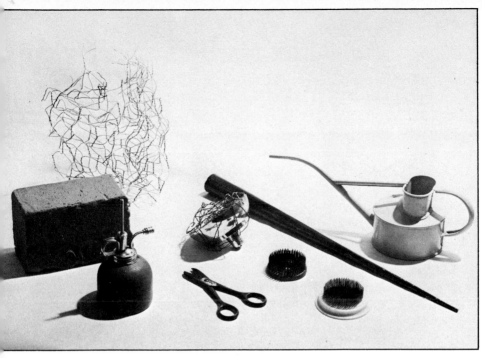

1 Oasis, chicken wire, atomizer, stub scissors, candle cup, pin-holders, cone and watering can

2 Mechanics for chicken wire base. First stage: Crumple wire and bend ends inwards

3   Second stage: wire ready for placing

4   Third stage: chicken wire reaching right down to base of bowl, over the top and secured at handles

5 Flower festival at St John the Baptist, Great Gaddesden. Cream and white
flowers with mixed foliage including cow parsley, hemlock and stripped lime

6 Flower festival at St John the Baptist, Great Gaddesden. Hanging wall plaque of stripped lime and mixed orange and cream flowers. The lovely arrangement on the radiator should have had trails of ivy or leaves to hide the air vents. I was responsible as the artistic director for the omission – let this be a warning!

7 Chancel decorations for St John the Baptist, Great Gaddesden. Pair of pedestals united by a garland on the altar rail. All in pale cream, yellow and white. See page 53

8 Flower festival at the parish church of St John the Baptist, Stanbridge. Garland of mixed foliage and summer flowers. For details, see page 53

9 Flower festival at St John the Baptist, Stanbridge. Flower ball inserted into a macramé base. See page 66

10   Pulpit decoration from St John the Baptist, Great Gaddesden, flower
festival, showing excellent use of the pulpit as a focal point for the festival. All the
flowers were white and pale yellow. For details, see page 61

11   Pulpit decoration for the flower festival at St John the Baptist, Stanbridge.
See page 60

12   Flower festival at St John the Baptist, Stanbridge. Mixed summer flowers
forming a garland. For details, see page 53

13　Pew end at St John the Baptist, Stanbridge. The flowers used are cow parsley, pink roses, pink sweet william and pink single spray chrysanthemum

church, on the other hand, can be enhanced by small garden flowers combined with hedgerow material.

Then think about colour, particularly if the background is a wall. For instance, grey stone soaks up colour more than stone of a pinkish hue. Screens and panelling of wood provide a good background for strong oranges and yellows, or an all-white group. If the colour chosen is white, make sure that you choose a variety of flowers to give different shades and textures. It is surprising how varied 'white' can be. Remove some of the foliage from white shrubs, for example philadelphus. Lilac lasts better if all the leaves are stripped. Many churches have brightly coloured curtains and carpets, or even decorative tiles. If the flower arrangement is near any of these, pick up the predominant colour. This helps to make the arrangement part of the building as a whole rather than a separate decoration. When these details are clear in your mind, you can begin to think about other aspects of your decorating.

CHOICE OF CONTAINER

Chapter 2 explains how desirable it is to use containers suitable to the building. It is also necessary to choose a container to suit the flowers which you are going to use, or, as the case may be, flowers to suit the container of your choice. Copper or brass is very good with strong colours, and a white or gilded urn looks marvellous filled with white or cream material. If the flowers hide the container, there is no problem.

LIGHTING

Do consider the lighting carefully. Blues and mauves are quite lost in artificial light, so use them only when there is plenty of natural light.

Some churches have excellent spot lights, which are a great help. Far fewer flowers will be needed. Where, on the other hand, lighting is poor, bold, strong colours are good, and so is white against a dark background. Lighting is so important that flower guilds ought to press for good lighting to show up the more important flower arrangements.

PROPORTION

When the flower arranger talks about proportion she means the relating of the flowers and the container to one another to make a balanced whole. If the container is to be seen when the arrangement is complete, the flowers must be at least one and a half times the height of the container. It does not matter if the flowers are far taller, but they must not be shorter! Everyone will have seen huge vases over the tops of which peer little short heads! However well the flowers are arranged, the proportion will always be wrong.

If a large heavy container is used, there must be flowers or foliage of sufficient visual strength to balance it. In photograph 22 you will see how my beautiful copper urn (a converted tea urn), which is tall and heavy, was used for a mixed arrangement. The lightness of the narcissi and daffodils was offset by large branches of lilac and some gladioli. Had only narcissi and daffodils been used with foliage the balance would have been wrong. There would have been too much emphasis on the urn. If the arrangement is to be a low one or one which hides the vase, any low, wide–topped conatiner will do. If you are using only spring flowers, which are by their nature light, then use a more delicate type of container: this will ensure good proportion.

COLOUR GROUPING

Flowers arranged in churches have to be seen from some distance. What looks right in a small room may be totally lost in a church. The way to make the greatest impact with flowers is to group your colours well. Remember that very light or very dark flowers stand out and hold your eye: therefore the way you use them will give shape to the arrangement. For instance, if you place very light flowers high up in the vase and gradually bring them down over the front and over to the sides this shape will be clearly seen. The darker flowers and leaves appropriately placed will give emphasis and depth.

If you are using shades of one colour, get some of the deep range in the middle and let the paler colours flow out from it. Mixed colours are always more difficult to arrange, but at certain times of the year you may have no option. Then the trick is to group the various colours together before you put anything into the container. Then pick out some light flowers and make a shape with them. Next use the very dark ones in the same way. You should now have the skeleton of the overall shape. You can then fill in the skeleton keeping other tones and colours together. If you dot odd colours about then, no matter how good the outline is, the final arrangement will have no definite shape or form and certainly will not be seen from a distance.

LINE

It is hard to define the exact meaning of 'line' in flower arranging. In this book it is used to describe shapes and rhythm formed by the careful placing of plant material and the use of colour groups. In large massed arrangements lines and curves are produced so as to emphasize the overall shape of the group. For example, I wanted the design of the construction arrangement shown in colour plate 2 to be loose and flowing, but it could easily have become a muddle had a clear line not been planned from the beginning. This line was achieved by keeping types of material together, using them to form a pattern, and getting clear lines and shapes from colour grouping. The pale cream roses were placed so that those in bud were high up, with those more fully open coming down through the middle to the base. The white philadelphus formed a clear outline curving from left to right, and the variegated periwinkle, providing the darkest colour, was placed very carefully to accentuate the shape required. When the outline and central shape were completed the other material was added.

A great deal can be learned about line by studying Japanese flower prints and the Ikebana School of flower arranging. It is a good discipline, as it not only makes one economical in the use of material but also teaches one to search out interestingly shaped branches and flowers. It is especially good for me because I am inclined to lash out and create far bigger arrangements than are always desirable!

CHOICE OF MATERIAL

When you have planned the colouring of your arrangement, collect your material together 24 hours ahead. If you are picking garden flowers, choose some in bud and some more open. Never pick fully open flowers: they will not last. Pick some stems which bend to the right and others which bend to the left; and, of course, some straight. It is easier to arrange uneven numbers, so three or five roses are better than two or four. Choose clearly defined leaves like hostas or bergenias, as well as good background foliage. Try to visualize roughly how much material is needed, and pick a little more in case some fades. When the material is well conditioned, place it in buckets of warm water and allow it 24 hours to drink. Preferably do this in the church: the less ferrying there is of flowers the better.

When you are ready to start your arrangement, spread a dust sheet out on the floor in front of your vase. This saves clearing up endless mess later!

ARRANGING THE FLOWERS

Figs 30, 31 and 32 illustrate three of the stages leading up to the final

arrangement in the urn in photograph 22. There are many occasions
for which this formal church arrangement provides a good pattern. It
looks well on a stool against a pedestal.

Make sure that the chicken wire is correctly placed in your container
(see Chapter 3), and if you are using a cone, fix it firmly into the wire.
Then fill the cone and three-quarters fill the container.

Take your background material and put it in first. Try to avoid a
stiff triangular effect. Instead of starting with a stiff central piece, get
a fuller branch of foliage or blossom slightly off centre, and have pieces
bending well over each side and over the front. Use the cone to give
height to shorter flowers. Remember the hints given earlier concerning
proportion, and in particular that the tallest flower must be at least one
and-a-half times the height of the vase. I hate rules, but this one is vital.
The other vital rule is that large arrangements need to have a focal point,
or what we call a 'face'. This is provided by the careful placing of leaves
or large flowers. All the material should look as if it springs from this
'face'. I have too often seen a wide vase used as a window box with
flowers running along the edge as if they had been planted. The effect
is terrible.

When you are placing the material in the container try to envisage
some pieces forward, some back, and some recessed low down: this will
give depth and interest. When the outline is complete and you have got
a clear focal point, fill in with the rest of the material. When you have
finished, stand well back to look at the result of your labours. If you
have any doubts about it, you may find it a help to take a walk round
the churchyard and then come back and look again with new eyes. If
you are not satisfied with what you see, do not do what one is inclined
in a desperate way to do, that is stuff in more flowers. More often than
not the cure is to take something out! Make sure, however, that there
are no gaps, especially at the side. If the arrangement can be seen from
more than one angle, fill in a bit of the back with foliage. Finally, top
up the container with water, and, in the summer, also spray.

8

Decorating the Church

This chapter describes various ways in which a church can be decorated, in particular the mechanics of decorations such as garlands and pew ends. Some of the ideas which you will find here will be of use in the ordinary week by week provision of flowers in the building: others belong rather to the special occasions, including flower festivals, which are dealt with in later chapters.

GARLANDS

All church flower arrangers should learn how to make a garland. The mechanics are such as to make the foundation of the garland completely pliable, so that it can take any shape and be of any size which is required. In photograph 7 taken at a flower festival at Great Gaddesden you will notice how the two large pedestals were drawn together by the garland running along the rail, in this case forming a straight horizontal line. In photograph 8, on the other hand, the garland makes a needed curve.

Garlands are very easy to make and provide a useful way of employing unskilled labour! Elderly people enjoy the work, because they can make a garland sitting down. If shown how to start, they find it a very rewarding job.

Before you start making the garland, plan your colouring. If you are making a curved garland like the one shown in photograph 8, you may like to keep all the deep colours in the middle and shade out to paler ones at the ends: or you may want the colouring to be uniform. Whatever you decide, sort out the colours and plan accordingly.

Mechanics of a garland

There are four stages to the making of a garland, as follows:

1 Take a brick of *Oasis* and cut it into 12 pieces (Fig. 7).
2 Make a polythene 'sausage' wide enough to hold the pieces of *Oasis* by taking a black dustbin bag, cutting it into strips twice as wide

as the finished 'sausage', folding the long strip in half and machining along one edge (Fig. 8). If a long garland is needed, it will be necessary to join two or more strips together before folding and machining.

3 Push the pieces of *Oasis* down the entire length of the 'sausage', tying it between each piece: use the ties which are sold with plastic bags. Secure each end with long pieces of strong string, leaving the ends free, or with stub wires (Fig. 9).

4 Lay the 'sausage' on a work table and push the foliage and leaves into the *Oasis* (Fig. 10). If the garland is to be on a ledge, it may be easier to work *in situ*. In this case use the bits of string to tie the 'sausage' down onto the ledge. If the garland is to be circular, surrounding a pillar or the font, tie it tightly in position when complete, using the loose ends of the string to join the ends of the garland together. Then fill any gaps which may be visible.

A garland once completed must be sprayed at least once a day, as the plant material is in very small pieces of *Oasis*.

WIRING LEAVES AND MAKING RIBBON BOWS

For general purposes there is no need to back leaves with wire, but if you are making a very narrow garland for a very special occasion some of the leaves may have to be backed. In that case:

1 Take a piece of silver florist's wire or fine fuse wire and make a stitch through the back of the leaf, leaving the two ends (Fig. 11).

2 Take the two ends of wire and wind them carefully round the stem: the leaf can then be bound onto either a stub wire or a small twig (Fig. 12). If the leaf is bound onto fuse wire, the wire should be covered with gutta-percha.

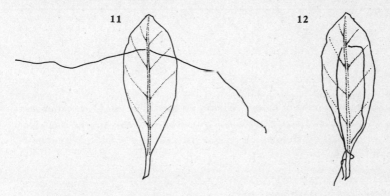

If you are putting loops of ribbon into a garland, as in photograph 10, the loops should be mounted on stub wire, as shown:

1 Take a length of ribbon and make two loops, pinching it into place (Fig. 13).

2 Wind a stub wire round the base, leaving two ends which will be pushed into the garland (Fig. 14).

PILLAR TOP DECORATIONS

When a church is being decorated for a special occasion it is a good idea to get flowers at a height, particularly if you want to draw attention to the carving of capitals or a beautiful roof. Whatever may be the particular reason for having them, flowers on the top of a pillar are very pretty. Where the capitals are carved the flowers must draw attention

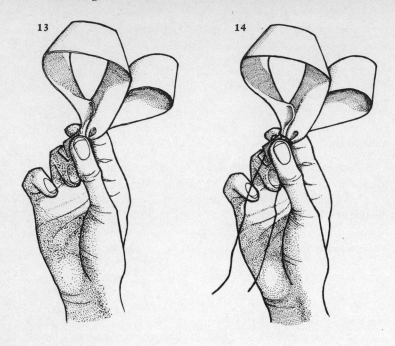

to the carving but not hide it. Where, on the other hand, the capitals are plain, trails of ivy or cow parsley or whatever else may be available can come well down the pillar. There are two ways of decorating the top of a pillar.

Pillars decorated with garlands

If there is only a small ledge round the top of the capital, a garland should be made long enough to go right round the ledge. In this case all that it necessary is to take the garland to the pillar and for one person to hand it up to another who, stationed on a ladder, will fix it in position, trying the two ends firmly together, and fill in any gaps.

Pillars decorated with triangles

You will sometimes find that there are on the top of a capital recesses roughly triangular in shape in the fluting of the arcading which springs from the top of the pillar, and these recesses may be large enough to hold pieces of *Oasis*. When using this method of decoration start by placing tinfoil so as to protect the stone in the recesses where the *Oasis* will be. Then proceed as follows:

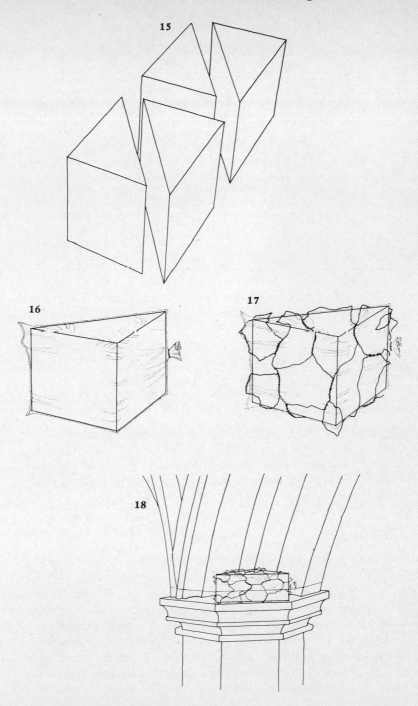

15

16

17

18

19

1 Cut a brick of wet *Oasis* into four triangles (Fig. 15).

2 Put each triangular piece into a plastic bag and secure it (Fig. 16).

3 Surround the bag with chicken wire and secure it with stub wire (Fig. 17).

4 Place a bag into a recess at each corner of the capital. Encircle the capital with string, threading it through the chicken wire on each bag so as to prevent it from falling forwards (Fig. 18).

5 Push the flowers and foliage into the *Oasis* so as to form a decoration of the size and shape required (Fig. 19).

Whichever method you use to decorate capitals the effect when complete should be that of a necklace of flower material encircling the top of the pillar (photograph 12). The decoration must not be heavy or irregular in size. It is essential to spray with water at least once a day, twice in hot weather.

PEW ENDS

The florist's term 'pew end' is used to describe a flower decoration hung on the end of a pew: you will see one in photograph 13. They are usually hung on the outsides of the pews on each side of the nave and can of course be used in aisles and chapels as well. They provide a useful way to taking colour from one end of the building to the other.

Nowadays sheaves of flowers for funerals are often made up onto a plastic holder shaped rather like a little dustpan, the back being designed to hold a block of *Oasis*. Rescue these when the funeral flowers have died: they provide invaluable mechanics for pew ends.

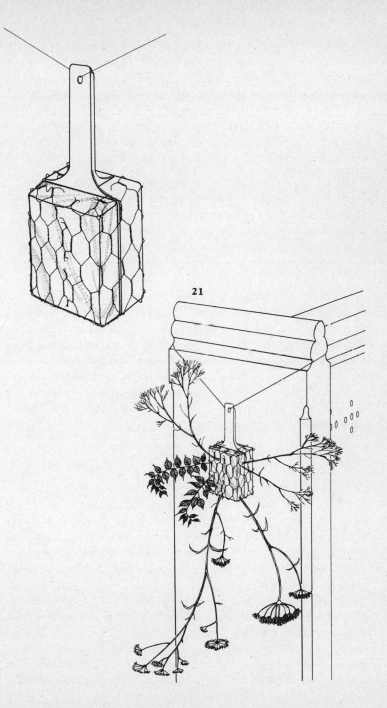

The pew end is made as follows:

1 Place a piece of wet *Oasis* in a plastic container and wrap chicken wire right round the container to stop the *Oasis* from falling forwards; then thread string through the hole in the handle of the container and tie it to the end of the pew (Fig. 20).

2 Push the plant material into the *Oasis* to form the required shape (Fig. 21). Make sure that the flowers do not stick out too far, remembering that at wedding and flower festivals there will be many people moving between the pews and they will knock against a pew end if it is too prominent.

Pew ends sometimes drip while they are being arranged, so before you start work put a piece of polythene on the floor underneath. This is absolutely essential in the case of a wooden or carpeted floor.

SCREENS

A carved screen seldom needs flowers, which may detract from its own beauty. There are, however, some special occasions when flowers on the screen are an advantage; for example, as a way of achieving extra height. Garlands may be used in a restrained way, or pew end holders containing small bouquets. Some churches have metal containers specially made to hang onto a screen. I remember seeing these used in a Hertfordshire church filled with spring flowers for Easter, and the effect was charming. The great thing to remember is that if the screen is delicately carved flowers must take second place.

PULPITS

The pulpit is one of the focal points of a church, but will only be decorated at special festivals. Before you start decorating the pulpit, decide exactly what the purpose of the flowers is to be. Is it to draw attention to the beauty of the pulpit itself, as by accentuating carvings? Or is the pulpit not a very attractive one and to be treated as a background for the flowers? Once you have decided you can plan your design accordingly.

Photographs 10 and 11 show pulpits decorated for flower festivals. Photograph 11 is of the pulpit at Stanbridge. You will notice the garland made to run along under the top ledge, from which four more garlands hang down. Observe how the garlands are used to draw attention to the carving running round the pulpit. The colours were pale pinks shading off to white with green foliage. This pulpit had candelbra into which were placed candle cups filled with flowers in damp *Oasis.* Similar decorations could be made for Christmas (see Chapter 9) using a variety of evergreens, loops of red ribbon and spray chrysanthemums. All pulpit decorations need to be sprayed with water. Care must taken not to mark wooden pulpits.

Photograph 10, taken at a flower festival at Great Gaddesden, shows more complicated pulpit decorations. The little bouquets on the steps were removed for the Sunday sermon and then replaced. The flowers were pale cream shading into yellow and green.

This method of decoration is achieved in the following way:

1 Blocks of *Oasis* are placed on the stone steps and also on the floor alongside the steps. Those on the floor in containers are graduated in height. One block can be fixed on top of another by means of dowels. (Fig. 22).

2 Pew ends are prepared (as described above), string is threaded through the holes in the handles, and they are suspended from hooks

22

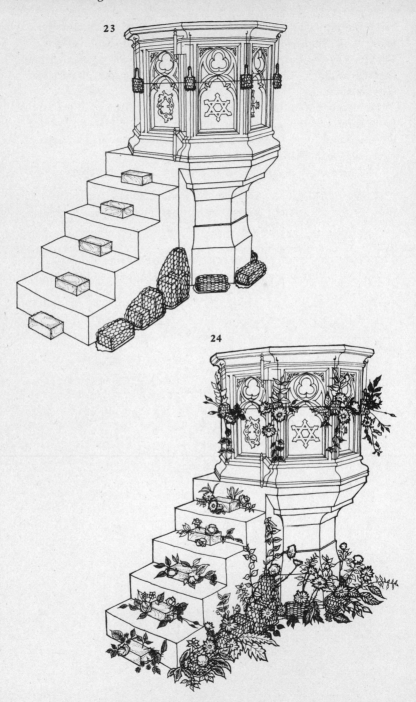

just below the ledge of the pulpit, a piece of string then being taken through the chicken wire at the back of each pew end and tied tightly round the pulpit so as to prevent any forward movement; the blocks of *Oasis* at the side are covered with 'cages' of chicken wire to give support (Fig. 23). *PLEASE NOTE:* There were already hooks in the pulpit in question; obviously the decorator must *not* put in hooks, but a piece of string can be tied tightly round the pulpit below the ledge and the pew ends suspended from that.

3 Fill with flower material (Fig. 24).

PORCHES

Whenever a church is decorated for a special occasion it is important to put flowers in the porch. After all it is the first place which visitors will see and flowers there will set the right atmosphere. Many porches have stone benches on one side or both sides of the door. A bench is a good foundation for a bank of flowers, or it can be decorated in a simpler way using mixed foliage arranged in troughs of *Oasis* with ivy hanging over the edge. Many porches have good window ledges which are ideal for flowers, and there is often a wooden roof from which flower balls can be hung.

PLAQUES

The term 'plaque' is used here to describe an arrangement which is to be hung on a wall. Some churches have no arches nor enough space to include pedestals and large vases, and the plaque is then a useful form of decoration. It is made in exactly the same way as a pew end (see above), the foundation being either the little plastic container illustrated in Fig. 20 or a large block of *Oasis* enclosed in a polythene bag, and it is hung from a beam or nail. The plaques at Whipsnade Church which you see in photograph 15 are good examples. This little church has a small nave with no arches and plaques hung from the light brackets are excellent. When plaques are hung on either side of the building they give colour to it. At Whipsnade they draw attention to the attractive light brackets. The garlands running underneath them are a feature for special occasions and emphasize the colouring of the plaques.

In a large church the plaques can be far bigger. I have made them of sprays of azalea and included lilies and stocks and roses. These were impressive and beautiful. The plaques which you see in photograph 6 taken at the Great Gaddesden flower festival included sprays of alchemilla and stripped lime.

WINDOW CILLS

Flowers are often arranged on window cills. If the cill tilts forward you must make a wedge to fit under the front of the container to keep it level and stop it toppling over.

If the window has very vivid colouring it may be difficult for the flowers to compete with it. In that case it is best to make the flowers part of the design and to pick up one or two of the srongest colours, using them boldly.

Plain glass in a window is an excellent background for delicate material like catkins, cow parsley and spring flowers. It will give enough light to show the form and detail of the material. If window cill arrangements are planned they should carry out the colour scheme of the rest of the building.

A window cill is likely to be high up, and therefore the container must be low: otherwise too much of it is visible. Bread baskets filled with *Oasis,* casseroles, pâté dishes, soup tureens and small copper preserving pans are excellent. At Harvest Thanksgiving a wide cill is an excellent place on which to make a composition using fruit and flowers.

FLOWER BALLS

When a church is being decorated for a special occasion it is a very attractive idea to have flower balls hanging either in arches or from ceilings or below lights. In small churches there may be very little space for pedestals or large vases, and then this form of decoration is ideal. Besides using them extensively at flower festivals I have made flower balls for country weddings with just cow parsley and daisies and they were enchanting. They are also excellent for making visitors look up and appreciate a beautiful roof or carvings.

If you get the mechanics right, flower balls are very easy to make.

1 Cut a brick of *Oasis* in half (Fig. 25).

2 Cut a piece of chicken wire. Place on it a half brick of *Oasis* in a polythene bag (Fig. 26).

3 Fold the chicken wire round the half block of *Oasis,* secure it and with a stub wire make a loop at the top; hang it on a hook, pulling it down once or twice to make sure that it is secure (Fig. 27).

4 Stuff flowers and pieces of foliage of the required length into the ball of *Oasis,* making sure that you keep a spherical outline and preferably using some trails of ivy, honeysuckle, alchemilla, cow parsley or other suitable material; when the outline is complete fill in gaps in the

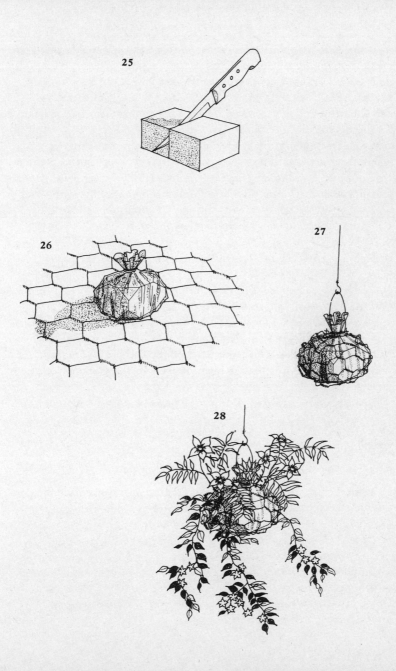

centre; you will have to turn the ball round continually with one hand and fill with the other (Fig. 28). The ball may be out of reach so that you have to stand on a ladder, in which case you will need a friend to pass flowers and pieces of the foliage to you.

If the balls are to be swung from a great height you will have to make them on the ground and haul them into position later. What I do is to find a place where I can stretch out a piece of string, sometimes between two pairs of step ladders, tie the mechanics onto it, and work from there. Afterwards I get a strong man with a good head for heights to hang the balls into position.

I was directing a flower festival at Eaton Bray in Bedfordshire where there is a beautiful church with a very high roof, and we wanted string thrown over the very high rafters to hold the flower balls. Believe it or not an archery champion lived locally and he shot the string over with an arrow. We then attached the completed flower balls to the string on the ground and pulled them up into position.

If the balls are going to hang at a great height, remember that it is the under parts which be seen and are important, while the top halves will hardly be visible.

You will see in photograph 9, showing the Stanbridge flower festival, that the flower balls are attached to the lights. These were rather ugly and we wanted to hide them. One of the local people was a macramé expert and she made a string foundation, similar to the kind used to hang flower pots, into which was inserted the half brick of Oasis in its polythene bag. This method can be recommended for churches fortunate enough to have a macramé expert.

Remember that flower balls must be sprayed at least once a day.

URNS

An arrangement in an urn is made in the following way:

1 Fill the urn with chicken wire so that it comes well over the top, push in a cone, and half fill both the urn and the cone with water (Fig. 29).

2 Make an outline with some of the material, letting some fall over the front of the urn (Fig. 30).

3 Still keeping within the original outline, fill in with more material; at this stage stand back to see where the gaps are (Fig. 31); continue filling in until the vase is finished; then top up both the urn and the cone with water (Fig. 32).

29

30

31

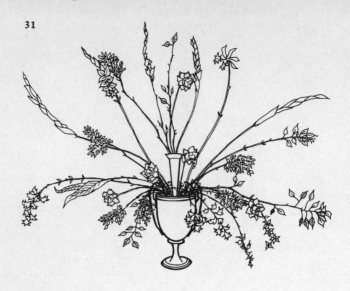

32

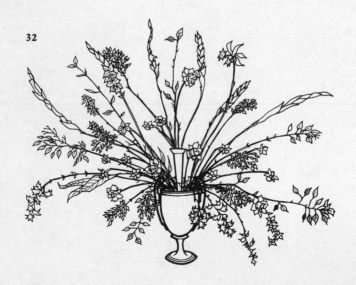

JUGS

I love arranging flowers in jugs, especially in country churches. There
are many attractive varieties, from plain earthenware to coloured
pottery and copper and brass. The jug by Michael Leach in colour
plate 2 is a particular favourite of mine. He calls it black, but I call it dark
brown! Remember when using a jug for flowers that it is itself important; therefore the handle must not be hidden and the flowers must
be in proportion to the height. When I am using this jug I need very
little chicken wire as the flowers are able to reach right down to the
bottom and quickly form a good foundation. In the arrangement
shown the lilies made a good background shape and stood up well
against the light, and the hellebores were excellent as I wanted
something to fall well over the edge. Weeping willow also makes lovely
flowing shapes. It lasts admirably if well conditioned in hot water.
A few stems of white spray chrysanthemum were added to give a
'face' to the arrangement.

PEDESTAL ARRANGEMENTS

Many people are terrified of arranging flowers on pedestals. There is no
reason for this provided that the mechanics are firm and reliable. As
explained earlier, the pedestal container must be wide-topped and deep
enough to hold heavy branches. When you have the chicken wire firmly
embedded in the container, pull it over the pedestal top. Then take two
pieces of strong string, thread one piece through the chicken wire so
that the string crosses the centre of the container and is carried underneath the pedestal top and tied; thread and tie the second piece of
string in the same way, but at right-angles to the first piece. This will
ensure that the container will not topple when filled with heavy
branches. Put in as many cones as you require, and then complete your
outline as described in the case of the urn on page 66.

If you look at photograph 5, of the beautiful pedestal arrangement
at the Great Gaddesden flower festival, you will see how a stiff
triangular effect has been avoided. The stripped lime sweeps up left and
right and the blossom flows well forward. The outline is light and 'airy',
but the lilies and gerberas give a good central focal point, so that the
arrangement was seen at a distance. Pedestal arrangements must include
some material of a substantial kind as well as light and flowing branches.

CONSTRUCTIONS

In Chapter 2, Containers, I have explained how constructions are made. The method of using them is as follows:

1 Fill each tier of the construction with *Oasis* (Fig. 33).

2 To give added support to the material make a cage of chicken wire to surround the tiers (Fig. 34).

3 Put in material to obtain an outline (Fig. 35) and then continue until the arrangement is complete. The completed construction is shown in colour plate 2.

33   34

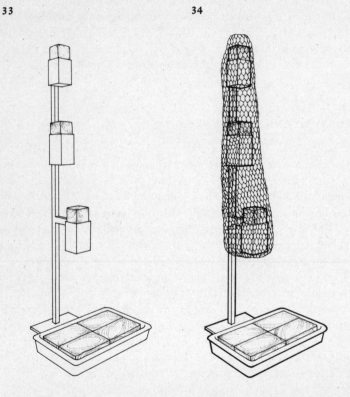

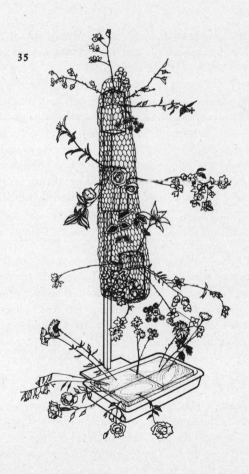

35

9 Festivals of the Church

CHRISTMAS

It is important to remember, particularly when planning flowers which are to stand in the chancel of a church, that the colours of the altar hangings vary according to the different seasons and festivals. White is used at Trinity, Christmas and other feasts of Christ, the Blessed Virgin Mary, Corpus Christi and feasts of virgins and confessors; red at Whitsuntide and for apostles and martyrs; green between Epiphany and Septuagesima and between Trinity Sunday and Advent; purple in Lent and Advent; and black on Good Friday and at masses and offices for the dead.

Most churches are without flowers during Advent, which therefore gives the flower guild plenty of time to prepare for Christmas, a festival to which everyone looks forward eagerly. This is a time, moreover, when it may well be possible to enlist help from outside the guild.

The style of decoration at Christmas should fit the character of the building. Old churches, particularly in the country, lend themselves to the traditional evergreens, including holly, and Christmas trees. Evergreens can be used in many ways. Garlands of holly, both plain and variegated, can be lightened by including in them bunches of honesty and loops of scarlet ribbon: see colour plate 4. These are charming in any kind of church. Holly balls can be made in the same way as flower balls and may also include red ribbon. They look enchanting hung in arches or from ceilings or lights.

Wall plaques (see colour plate 4) are easily made, whether one uses evergreens alone or mixed with spray chrysanthemums or scarlet carnations. If the building is large enough, a pedestal group is a great addition at Christmas time. If the church is a simple one, use plain or variegated holly for the background with branches whitened to resemble snow (I simply paint on white plastic paint.) Include honesty — this is more effective if it is well lit by a spot light — fir cones attached to stub wires, and, if the church can afford them, a few sprays of white chrysanthemums.

If the church which you are decorating is more sophisticated in style and includes gold colouring, a group in keeping with the background is appropriate. Aerosols of gold paint — readily available at Christmas — colour material well. Put down a dust sheet and collect onto it branches, fir cones, and dried material including seed heads of poppy and delphinium and spray them with gold. Collect other material like honesty, variegated holly, ivies and some golden spray chrysanthemums and create a large golden group. I do not, however, feel that a group of this kind is right in a small village church.

Another way of making a Christmas pedestal arrangement is to use evergreens with scarlet carnations and red poinsettias taken out of their pots and tied into polythene bags (see Chapter 6) and used as flowers. Three pots will be enough for most arrangements. If it is a huge arrangement, the poinsettias can be lashed onto strong sticks to give them height.

I am unashamedly sentimental and feel that Christmas trees are an essential part of Christmas decorations. A large one near the chancel is a lovely welcoming sight. If possible, try to keep the decorations to one colour scheme. If red and green are predominant, use them on the tree. The effect of the golden pedestal group described above would be enhanced by a tree decorated in gold and silver.

In a country church small Christmas trees on the window cills are simple and pretty. Some churches have a custom at Christmas (and also at Easter) of inviting members of the congregation to give a single lily in memory of some departed one. *Longiflorum* lilies are available at Christmas and look beautiful in Christmas groups. If some of these can be acquired, a pedestal at the altar arranged with lilies, spray chrysanthemums, honesty and some green is a great joy. If the church is one which has flowers on the altar, lilies and carnations are suitable because they both look and last well.

EASTER

After the starkness of Lent Easter provides a welcome opportunity to fill the church with flowers, representing the New Light coming into the world and the Rebirth of Spring.

The flower guild should plan a flower pool well in advance. One source of this will be the hedgerows, which, if Easter is not too late, will provide catkins and pussy willow (commonly called palm). Depending on the weather, the gardens may have daffodils, narcissi, hellebores and polyanthus. At least three weeks in advance have a look at forsythia and wild cherry blossom. If the buds are tight and green, cut sprays and bring them into a warm place to force them open. They take about three weeks in a coolish place, but a shorter time in a very warm room.

When the flower guild knows roughly how much material can be cut from hedgerows and gardens it must decide what to buy. Some lilies, both the beautiful white *longiflorum* and *arum*, add greatly to spring flower arrangements. They last well in water, but they are expensive. In connection with Christmas, the custom has been mentioned of members of the congregation donating lilies: if they do this, their gifts provide a useful addition to the pool. *Arum* lilies should be ordered several weeks before Easter, especially if they are to come from a local nursery. Do order leaves with the blossoms: they are so beautiful. White hyacinths are also well worth buying. Several grouped together give a good focal point to a mixed spring arrangement.

Many people find spring flowers disappointing when cut and arranged in a vase. It is helpful to imagine how they grow naturally, either in large clumps or as carpets spreading out to give solid masses of colour. When planted singly in rows with only the faces visible they appear stiff and unnatural. The same principle applies to vases of spring flowers. If daffodils or narcissi are placed singly all facing forwards the arrangement will appear 'spotty' and unnatural. Instead pick up a small bunch in your hand, put the flowers in the vase, and allow them to fall about quite naturally, some facing forwards and some turning away; the back or sideways view of daffodils is as pretty as the full face. Place some bunches in cones to give height, and some lower down in the chicken wire. If the bunches are grouped together they will give the needed splashes of colour and enable the arrangement to be seen far back in the church. If lilies or hyacinths have been bought, they will of course be a tremendous help. Five arum lilies and their leaves in a spring vase give a good focal point. A pedestal arrangement, especially in a large church or a cathedral, must include great boughs of blossom and some foiliage if it is to make any impact.

Window cills are excellent for spring flowers, especially if there is no coloured glass in the windows. Plain windows give enough light to show the form of catkins and spring flowers. Baskets are particularly suitable containers, as are copper troughs or bowls. Do include some trails of ivy: they look so pretty falling over the edge of the cill.

If there are plenty of helpers and there is enough material, pillar arrangements and flower balls look enchanting in small country churches as Easter time.

Some churches have special containers to hang on the screen or pulpit and these filled with daffodils and light foliage make the church look very festive. Do remember the porch. In the country a jug simply filled with sprays of forsythia, blossom or palm standing near the church door looks welcoming. So do spring flowers on a window cill or stone bench.

EASTER GARDENS

These are usually made by children with help from adults. They vary enormously in style and execution. The base of the garden must hold damp earth and moss: therefore it must be waterproof. Having selected a suitable site on the floor of the building, lay down layers of newspaper to cover the area which the garden is to occupy. On top of the newspaper place two layers of the strongest sort of polythene: the kind which builders use is the best.

Collect earth in buckets, and if possible enough moss to cover the garden. Collect twigs of catkin and pussy willow, small plants like Christmas primroses and grape hyacinths (depending upon the date of Easter), and some cut flowers, for example, daffodils and narcissi. Find some suitable and attractive stones with which to make the tomb, and some flat ones to form a path. Then cover the area of the garden with earth.

The tomb is the focal point of the garden. The rest of it must point to the tomb; so build it at a strategic point slightly right or left of the centre. The garden will be more interesting if it has different levels, so build up earth to get the tomb slightly higher than the surrounding area. There should be three plain wooden crosses behind the tomb. The path leading to the tomb gives emphasis to the design.

Use some of the twigs to make little trees, and clumps of plants or flowers to make the garden. Cut flowers should look as if they are growing, so include the leaves. To hold the flowers or plants use tiny containers pushed into the earth, or else *Oasis*, in either case covered with moss. Use the 'trees' carefully to give height and distance.

If the church is very small, an Easter garden can be mounted on a very large meat dish and put on a table. If it is possible to train a spot light on the garden, the effect is greatly improved.

WHITSUN

It is customary for churches to have red and white flowers at Whitsun. This is a difficult combination and normally I would not choose to have such a strong contrast. There are, however, ways of using these colours to advantage. The altar frontal will be red: therefore pedestals near the altar could feature bold groups composed of clashing scarlets, pinks and deep reds. These are extraordinarily effective at any time and particularly good with the red frontals. Flowers on the altar itself should be

white, and they will give a bold interpretation of this scheme. The
white flowers could be arranged with grey or variegated green foliage.
The red groups look best if they have very little foliage. Make them a
solid splash of red tones: but if you do want foliage then variegated or
grey has a softening effect, and does not give too strong a contrast.

If the flower guild particularly wants mixed arrangements of white
and red, the points made in Chapter 7, 'First Steps', on colour
grouping will be found helpful in creating an attractive shape.

HARVEST THANKSGIVING

Harvest time provides an opportunity to fill the church with colour.
The prettiest effect is achieved if flowers and fruit and vegetables are
used together in big arrangements. Fruit and vegetables provide a
marvellous range of colours and textures. They look less satisfactory
just piled in heaps on the floor.

Large pedestals can be arranged with foliage in autumn colours or
beech which has been preserved in glycerine. Leaves such as those of
paeonies and hostas can be used combined with flowers like dahlias,
late roses and rudbeckias; also sprays of fruit such as blackberries
(preserved in glycerine: see Chapter 5), tomatoes on their stems, hips,
old man's beard, and, as a central focal point, cauliflower wedged into
chicken wire and bunches of grapes attached to stub wires.

A wooden table is a good place upon which to build up a design of
flowers, fruit and vegetables, but in the case of a valuable table it is
essential before starting work to spread a sheet of polythene as a
protection for it. When flowers are used one must, of course, have a
container filled with water or *Oasis*. When the basic outline has been
made it should at an early stage be filled in with fruit or large material.
If plants are used they should be taken out of their pots and their
roots should be tied into polythene bags. In the pink harvest arrangement shown in colour plate 3 the large fern was in a plastic bag placed
in the vase and on the table behind the cauliflower a small fern was
treated in the same way and used with the fruit to make a complete
picture.

Window cills are excellent for staging mixed arrangements of flowers,
fruit and vegetables. If there are plenty of helpers it should be possible
to have garlands of berries and leaves round the font and the pulpit, and
to decorate the pew ends with flowers, old man's beard, blackberries
and hips. The effect is very attractive.

If your church is considering staging a flower festival, think about
combining it with Harvest Thanksgiving. This is a very suitable time.

10 ♄
Weddings, Christenings and Funerals

WEDDINGS

When a bride becomes engaged and is making plans for her wedding she will be well advised to visit without delay the incumbent of the church where she wishes to be married and to book the date with him, especially if she wants a Saturday in spring or summer, for weddings in churches are generally booked very early. If the bride is employing a professional florist, she too should be booked in good time. Popular churches and florists can be booked up nine months ahead, and some fashionable London churches may be booked as far as a year in advance. Remember that churches are usually without flowers in Advent and Lent. Flowers may be allowed for weddings, but usually on condition that they are removed immediately after the service.

May I suggest that if there are to be bridesmaids the colouring of their dresses should be given priority in the plans, and also that the colouring should take account of the decorations in the church? I realize that the bride will have to play this one very carefully as adult bridesmaids are usually keen to 'do their own thing', but if you can visualize the wedding group standing in the church for some time you will see that the patch of colour provided by the bridesmaids' dresses is a very striking feature. A carpet or a curtain or a highly coloured window may provide a background colour, and if the dresses can tone in or else provide a contrast the congregation will enjoy a beautiful picture. I prefer tones of one colour: I find that a good contrast is always difficult to achieve.

When the colouring has been decided, the next step is to plan the flowers. A large factor will be the amount of money available. Another will be the season and what flowers will be out in the garden. The flowers must be discussed with the incumbent. Some incumbents are happy to have the church filled with flowers, but others limit them to certain areas.

If there is an active flower guild the bride may be content for the members to arrange all her flowers. In that case they will plan the colouring with her and make a charge for each arrangement. Brides should appreciate how much time and trouble flower guild members take in planning and arranging wedding flowers. Many chairmen of flower guilds spend hours matching colours, raiding gardens and combing hedgerows, as well as visiting markets and, at the end of all this, charge only a very small amount. If on the other hand the bride chooses to employ a professional florist, or has friends to arrange her flowers, she must inform the flower guild. I know from experience the great embarrassment of arriving at a church armed with flowers, having been engaged by the bride to provide several pedestal arrangements, only to find the flowers already being done by the flower rota lady because the bride had failed to notify the flower guild of her plans. If possible, plan the church flowers about three months ahead, so that nearer the day whoever is in charge of the flowers can arrange for picking or buying without a last minute discussion.

If the church is a large one it is much better to concentrate on several big pedestal groups rather than a number of small ones scattered about the building. If you are not very familiar with the building, arrange to meet the verger (if there is one) or someone else who can show you round and tell you what pedestals and vases the church owns and what sort of lighting is available. There are often spotlights to illuminate the chancel and some churches have them in other areas as well. Information about spotlights is valuable if the building is a dark one. Good lighting means that the congregation can see pedestals at a distance and fewer flowers are needed. This is important when expense is a problem. I suggest that there should be a pedestal arrangement beside the altar, and another one nearer to the congregation. The lectern is not used at weddings and many incumbents allow it to be moved to provide a good place for a pedestal arrangement or a large vase. Some incumbents do not allow flowers on the altar; but if flowers are allowed there they provide an excellent focal point to catch the eye of the congregation. If it can be afforded, a vase in the porch or somewhere near the entrance gives a welcoming effect.

Many brides, particularly if they have access to large gardens, like the church to be lavishly decorated. If the congregation is going to fill the building, there may be very little floor space for pedestals and vases. This is an occasion for keeping flowers at a height. Pillar arrangements, flower balls, pew ends and wall plaques often provide a splendid and pretty solution to the problem. In a country church they can be made with attractive small material from gardens and hedgerows. In a large

and formal church more sophisticated and exotic flowers can be used.
If there are suitable window cills, they will make good places for flowers.

For an early July wedding I once made an arch of white 'Iceberg'
and 'Pascali' roses and white border carnations mixed with lime
flowers, alchemilla and cow parsley. The church had a chancel screen
with a pointed arch in the middle. I made a 'garland sausage' (see
Chapter 8), fairly wide to encase small pieces of *Oasis,* and tied it up
one side of the arch, over the top and down the other side. The garland,
being made of such light and pretty material, showed up beautifully
against the rather pale wooden screen.

CHRISTENINGS

The flower guild would not normally arrange special flowers for a
christening service, but the incumbent it usually very happy for parents
to provide flowers if they so wish. Some incumbents allow a garland to
be placed on the ledge surrounding the font provided that a sufficiently
wide area is left free to reach the water and christen the baby. The
garland will take the form of a horseshoe. Chapter 8 explains how to
make a garland. If *Blue Tak* is placed at intervals along the ledge and
the underside of the garland is pressed down hard onto it, the garland
should be safely anchored for the brief time that it has to be there. *Blue
Tak* does not mark stone: this is important. For a garland made for this
occasion, small, pale pretty flowers are recommended, such as grape
hyacinths, daffodils and crocuses with leaves for the spring; lilies of the
valley, small roses, pinks and any other small garden flowers for the
summer; while leaves, berries and little dahlias are light and pretty
in the autumn.

When the garland is finished and placed on the ledge, light trails
of ivy or alchemilla or cow parsley depending on the season can be
pushed into it so as to trail over the side. If there are steps leading up
to the font this form of decoration can be emphasized by making
another garland to encircle the base of the font, resting on the steps.
There is often a window conveniently near to the font and, provided
that there is not too much coloured glass, a vase of flowers on the cill
carrying out the colours of the garland makes an attractive addition to
the decorations. Alternatively, a large pedestal arrangement near the
font provides a good background.

FUNERALS

Flowers at a funeral bring joy and solace to the bereaved. I suggest that

there should be flowers either on the altar or near to it on a large
pedestal; also that there should be one large vase or pedestal arrangement near the coffin, and that this is probably enough. There is no
reason why the colours should be sombre, but most families prefer
white or pale flowers. Nowadays many families ask that instead of
wreaths there should be cut flowers made up into sheaves. These, if
they can all be placed together somewhere inside the church or in the
porch, make a splash of colour which the mourners see as they enter
the building. After the service they can be sent to old people's homes
and hospitals. It is wise to arrange beforehand for some member of the
family to remove the cards from the flowers before they are taken away.

MEMORIAL SERVICES

Many memorial services are held several weeks after a cremation and
take the form of a thanksgiving for the life of the person concerned.
The family often wish the service to be a joyous occasion, especially if
it is for someone who has reached old age after a full and happy life. In
such a case the family, particularly if they are flower lovers or keen
gardeners, may like to have lots of flowers in the church, and often
their friends are prepared to help to decorate it as a tribute to the
departed.

MEMORIAL FLOWERS

Many people like to arrange flowers in a church in memory of a relation
or friend. In the case of someone lost in war, the flowers may be placed
in front of the War Memorial. In other cases there may be a suitable
ledge under a plaque or a memorial window. In such a case the flowers
are a personal tribute, not intended to be seen at a distance as part of
the general decoration of the building. This being so, it is entirely a
matter of personal choice what flowers are used. As was described
earlier, there is a custom in some churches of asking members of the
congregation at Christmas and at Easter to donate a lily in memory of
some loved person; this is a charming way of building up a good pool of
flowers for those festivals.

11 Flower Festivals: Planning and Publicity

PLANNING

Over the past 25 years flower festivals have been held in churches throughout the British Isles. The occasion is one when the whole building is decorated with flowers, sometimes quite simply, sometimes in a very elaborate way, and is for several days kept open to the public, usually from about 10.00 am until about 8.00 pm. Sometimes a charge is made for admission, or for a programme; or containers – carboys are excellent for this purpose – are placed about the church in the hope that visitors will contribute generously in appreciation of what they have seen. The object is not, however, simply to make money, though the festival is a very good way of raising funds; more importantly, it generates interest in the church itself, both locally and futher afield. It is a great attraction to visitors from overseas; Americans in particular are fascinated, both by the flowers themselves and by the beauty of our church buildings, which they might not otherwise see.

There are certain essentials to a successful flower festival and the first is the wholehearted enthusiasm of the incumbent and at least three other people, one of whom should be an experienced flower arranger. They form the nucleus about which must be gathered the team needed to organize and run the event.

A festival needs to be planned well in advance of its date, nine months at least and preferably a year, and a date must be chosen with care so that the festival does not clash with other local events, particularly other fund-raisers. It follows that the intention to have a festival must be publicized early; for instance, the diocesan office should be told, and also other churches in the locality, which may have a similar event in mind.

The festival committee will need to have sub-comittees, meeting at fairly regular intervals throughout the year. One way and another there will be a great deal to be done and much of the work will be hard and unglamorous, particularly during the actual week of the festival – filling buckets, picking and conditioning plant material, fetching and carrying generally. Remember that a festival usually lasts for three days, from Friday to Sunday, and sometimes over Monday as well. The previous Monday and Tuesday must be given over to picking and conditioning and Wednesday evening and Thursday to staging: so there is a good week's work.

Having talked about the snags let me hasten to say that I have been involved in a great many flower festivals, directing them in such diverse places as St Albans Abbey, which is vast, and Whipsnade Church, which is tiny, and I have always found the work rewarding and inspiring.

Time and work can be saved by good forward planning by the committee, and this chapter deals with that aspect of the festival. I shall describe the functions of the key officers of the committee and the various sub-committees and every detail of planning, but obviously in the case of a small church the size of the operation will be scaled down and carried out by fewer people. For the sake of convenience and ignoring the Sex Discrimination Act I have assumed that, the incumbent apart, the participation in the running of the festival will be female! In fact many jobs are often done by men, who may well be numbered among the flower arrangers.

The chairman

Whether the idea of having a flower festival originates with the incumbent himself, or whether someone else suggests it to him, it is usually he who will make preliminary inquiries to ascertain the practicability of having a festival and who will appoint the chairman of the organizing committee. The chairman will then constitute the basic committee.

The chairman will need to know about flower arranging and the conditioning of flower material, but she need not be herself a very expert flower arranger, because the actual designing and directing of the festival is the task of the artistic director. The chairman will be responsible for overseeing all sub-committees, for checking every aspect of the festival, including the conditioning of plant material and the staging in festival week; in other words, for co-ordination generally.

The secretary

The secretary's task will be to deal with the very large amount of paper work which will have to be done and the endless queries on the telephone. It is an advantage to have as secretary someone who is available at least for part of the time during the day, and it is essential that she is available on the telephone.

The publicity officer

This is another key person in the festival. She will be responsible for publicity for the festival throughout the previous year. It is very desirable to have an imaginative person – possibly quite young – with new and original ideas.

The artistic director

When the festival committee has been formed it must appoint an artistic director. She need not be a professional florist: I remember a particularly beautiful festival in a small local church which was directed by the incumbent's wife. She knew and loved every part of the building and her feeling for it was expressed in the design, which has had a lasting effect on my own approach when directing a festival.

The artistic director's job is to plan the whole festival. She must decide where there are to be flowers and on a colour scheme for the whole building, and she must indicate the location of the individual arrangements on a plan of the church. She must be on hand to give advice when staging is taking place. She must help over the buying of flowers, conditioning them and arranging them. Also, she will be expected to attend some of the committee meetings before the festival is staged so as to advise.

It is important to realize that not only must the artistic director be a skilled flower arranger, but she must also be a person of originality and vision capable of designing a scheme appropriate to the building as a whole. Nor does her task end there. Flower festivals use every sort of flower arranger, some skilled, some very nervous and inexperienced, some – I have to say it! – ruthless and bossy! The director must keep these various talents under her control. In some cases she must encourage and help; in others she must make sure that the more dominant workers do not discourage the timid! I have worked at festivals with brilliant directors who have insisted on their plans being carried out to the last petal – in such a ruthless and rigid way as to make the festival an unhappy occasion instead of the joyous event which it should be. There has to be some degree of compromise and there must be tact and kindness. Having said all this I now feel very embarrassed as I know that some of the people with whom I have worked over the years will be shaking their heads and saying, 'Good heavens!

Does she think that she is the paragon whom she describes?' The answer is that of course I am not: I am describing the director we would all like to be!

When the committee invites somone to design and direct the festival it should bear in mind the fact that the job calls for months of work, and should expect to pay a fee. Many artistic directors are happy to give their services free, especially if the festival is to be held at the director's own church; but where the director has no personal connection with the church and is a working professional florist she may not be able to afford to give up all the time required, and then it is up to her to say what her fee will be and for the committee to decide whether it can afford to employ her. The director must say at the start exactly how much time she is prepared to give to the festival and what she requires the secretary to do for her.

The treasurer

The treasurer is in sole charge of all money transactions and responsible for receiving and settling all the bills.

The catering chairman

The catering for the festival will be most satisfactory if someone is appointed as catering chairman and then forms her own sub-committee. The task of this sub-committee is to plan and provide the catering for the general public during the festival. In fact it is very often possible to get the Mothers' Union with the help of the Young Wives to take on this important job.

Sub-committees

The artistic director will work with the main festival committee. The other key officers whom I have described may want help and in that case they can form their own sub-committee composed generally of friends whom they are accustomed to working with. I am much opposed to large and complicated committees. It is much better to have small groups of hard-working people who are used to working together.

Aims of the festival

Once the flower festival committee has appointed its officers the incumbent will ask the chairman to call a meeting to discuss exactly what sort of festival is planned. Some small churches decide only to decorate the church with flowers; larger ones may be more ambitious and incorporate exhibitions of, for example, embroidery, crafts or pictures; or may decide to stage some special feature as an added attraction. The aims and plans of the committee should be quite clear so that the artistic director can be informed. It is important for her to know about any special features which are contemplated before she prepares her plan. In fact the artistic director is usually invited to attend this first meeting.

Cost

The other important matter to be discussed at the first meeting of the committee is the question of cost. Publicity, postal charges, flowers, *Oasis* and many other items mount up only too quickly. Many festivals are financed by fundraisers – coffee mornings, jumble sales, etc – held well in advance, the proceeds going straight into the flower fund. Otherwise the initial cost has to be met from church funds.

A flower festival will not be a financial success if the outgoings are too high. Expenditure on publicity is essential and there is bound to be a bill for postage. Great care should therefore be taken not to overspend in purchasing flowers.

The artistic director's plan

At the time when I was first asked to direct a flower festival I had never seen one! I had as a professional florist of course worked in churches for many years, and this was helpful: but a flower festival seemed very daunting. In a way, however, to have no preconceived ideas was a help.

I decided to use flowers so as to accentuate the beauty of the building, concentrating on carefully planned colour ranges. This was 20 years ago and today the festival which I directed then would probably be thought to be very naive. Nevertheless, I have remembered the lessons which I learned then and they have given me the confidence to tackle enormous projects. So, to the new artistic director I would say: 'Take heart, plan carefully, and make sure that your festival chairman and committee are in complete agreement.' This team working in harmony – their sole object being to make the church building more beautiful and to attract people to it – will establish the right atmosphere, and that will last even through the odd dramas which appear as staging day approaches!

In the case of a small festival the artistic director will be able to make her plan unaided. In the case of a cathedral or a very large parish church she may need some assistance. When in 1977 I was asked to direct a flower festival in St Albans Abbey, one of the largest of our cathedrals, I realized that I must have a design committee. At first as I sat in various parts of the building I was terrified by the vastness of the task which I had undertaken. By degrees, however, I came to see that the building could be split up into distinct areas which could be individually planned – the nave, the aisles, the choir, the transepts, the presbytery, the chapels and so on. So I gathered together a group of friends whom I knew to be very experienced in decorating for flower festivals and I was able to explain to each my plan for a particular part of the building. They then carried out the plan, though subject to my overall control. It was a great assistance to me to have the benefit of their ideas and knowledge both throughout the planning stage and during the festival itself.

The first consideration in making the plan is colour, and this must to some extent be dictated by the building itself. St Albans Abbey provides a good example. The largest area which I had to consider was the nave, a dominant feature of which is the medieval paintings which adorn a number of the columns of the arcades. In some lights the paintings seem to be predominantly pink, in others terra cotta. At first I found it hard to decide upon colour scheme for the flowers. By chance I saw on television the ballet of *Othello* in which the principals wore costumes in shades of brown, cream and terra cotta, and this decided me to settle on those colours for the nave! We had vast constructions against the pillars, while flower balls hung from the lights in the arches of the arcades drew the eye up to the superb wooden ceiling. Towards the nave altar the colouring was gradually shaded down into pale cream and white. The effect was very dramatic. It is a good idea to include green in a colour scheme. It is an effective foil to other colours. Moreover, the material is generally obtainable free! At St Albans we had banks and pedestals of green of every shade in the aisles and the contrast with the other colours which I have described was splendid.

When you have decided on your colour scheme, then think about composition. A flower festival provides an opportunity to paint a picture with flowers. As an artist uses vertical and horizontal lines, so should the artistic director. Constructions and pedestals provide vertical shapes, garlands horizontal. Flower balls give another dimension. Notice how in photograph 7, of the flower festival at Great Gaddesden, the two pedestals at the altar are joined together by the garland running along the altar rail.

Particular care must be taken over colour and composition in a case in which it is decided to include a special exhibition – for example, of crafts or embroidery – in the festival. The best course is to keep the special exhibition in one part of the building, such as a chapel or transept, and under its own director. If the special exhibition is intermingled with the flowers, the two directors must work together.

Flowers themselves may be used to illustrate special themes and so add interest to the festival. I have, for instance, seen biblical texts and local history brilliantly illustrated with flowers. The difficulty with special exhibitions generally is that, unless they can be confined to one part of the building, the concept of an overall colour scheme and design, intended to accentuate the beauty of the building, may be lost. This is because each set piece in the exhibition is the expression of an individual idea and symmetry suffers accordingly.

Not all church buildings are beautiful in themselves, so that sometimes the plan must aim not at accentuating features but at hiding them.

Before the artistic director plans her scheme in detail she must be provided with a ground plan of the building on which every important feature is marked. Very often there is already such a plan in existence and it can be photocopied. Several copies will be needed. The artistic director will need two or three, and the secretary should have one. It is as well to have some spare copies.

The artistic director must go round the building with a copy of the plan and mark in on it the position of every flower arrangement, garland, pew end decoration and so on. Great care must be taken to ensure that the plan is accurate and I find that the artistic director needs an assistant. The artistic director calls out the details and the assistant marks the plan accordingly. It will usually be found necessary to start with a draft plan and to 'fair copy' it. It is very helpful to use different colours for different types of arrangement, one colour for pedestals, another for garlands and so on, and to have a key to the colours at the side of the plan. By the use of colours a better idea is given by the completed plan of what the church will look like.

Each item should be given a number and it is important that the sequence of the numbers on the final version of the plan should follow the route which the public will take when moving through the church. If, for example, the public are admitted through a porch at the west end of the building, the numbering will start with the arrangements in the porch. Remember that the plan is completed well in advance of the festival and that from it the allocation of positions is made. The artistic director's nightmare is that on staging day Mrs Smith and Mrs Brown will each appear laden with flowers determined that she has been instructed to do pedestal no. 3!

Allocation of arrangements

When the plan is complete and it can be seen exactly now many arrangements there are to be the artistic director must decide how they are to be allocated. If there is a regular flower guild it is important to ask first of all how many of its members wish to take part in the festival and how many and what sort of arrangements they want to undertake.

Source of flower arrangers

Do not bring in outside help until you are satisfied that full use is being made of the local regular flower arrangers. It is very sad if any of them feel ousted. If they are happy and there are still positions to be filled, the committee must decide who else is to be asked. Nowadays many neighbouring churches, including churches of different denominations, help each other at flower festivals, and a letter written to local clergy asking for volunteer flower arrangers usually produces a good response. There may also be local organizations like Women's Institutes, Townswomen's Guilds, Horticultural Societies and Flower Clubs, all of which are invaluable as sources of decorators. It saves time and trouble to have a printed or photo-copied letter to which is attached a slip on which are listed particulars of the arrangements which need to be done, for example, pedestals, pew ends, garlands, etc. The recipient of the letter is asked to tick her choice and to send the slip back to the secretary. The letter should be sent to every parish and organization which has offered help. It is sensible to give a closing date for the return of the slips, because many people are very vague about time! When the slips have been returned the artistic director with the help of the secretary can then allocate any positions which have not yet been filled.

PUBLICITY

One of the most important aspects of a flower festival is good, original and well-organized publicity, planned well in advance. Too often a beautiful festival has had very few visitors simply because people outside the parish have not known of its existence. I have been amazed sometimes at the attitude towards choosing a publicity officer of flower festival committees. I have heard remarks like 'Old Mr Bloggins might do it', regardless of whether old Mr Bloggins is interested or has any ideas! Choose your publicity representatives very early on and if possible recruit some young people. Youth clubs will often work very hard, not only delivering pamphlets, etc, but also producing ideas. If you can get the members of a youth club keen and interested they will during staging week do such things as driving decorated cars or vans, touring neighbouring towns and villages with loud halers giving details of the festival, and walking up and down the streets with sandwich boards with festival notices. Original ideas like these attract the public's attention. Then there are many more conventional methods of publicity such as posters, pamphlets, notices and programmes.

Posters

Posters in two sizes are needed, a few very big ones and a number of smaller ones which can be conveniently displayed in shops and windows. Shops do not like very large ones. The large posters need to be printed on a good clear background. The fluorescent ones are excellent. A bright pink or yellow background with black lettering is easily seen. Do limit the lettering to basic essentials like FLOWER FESTIVAL in huge print, with details of opening times and a large arrow pointing in the direction of the church. These posters ought to be placed at cross-roads, and if the church is in an isolated village try to get some of them sited at stategic points near junctions on main roads. There should also be some huge posters in the churchyards. Small posters for windows, to be legible, should have the minimum of information; for example, FLOWER FESTIVAL, opening times, special features (if any) and catering arrangements. I have often seen posters with a life history plus little drawings – illegible from any distance!

Pamphlets

Simple pamphlets to be left at neighbouring churches and put into the letter boxes of houses in neighbouring villages are excellent publicity.

Programmes

Each flower arrangement is given a number and this is printed in the festival programme with the name of the flower arranger beside it. If the church is of historic interest, it is worth while printing a short history at the beginning of the programme. Programmes will be available for sale at the church door, but they can also be sold a week or two in advance of the festival as a means of publicity for it. Bitter experience teaches one, however, that there is no point in spending money on expensively produced programmes. They simply do not sell. The public wants the basic information and will only pay accordingly! Do, indeed, be economical not only over programmes but over all printed material, except for the very large posters which must be of a high quality.

AA and RAC signs

The Automobile Association and the Royal Automobile Club will supply excellent signs simply saying FLOWER FESTIVAL with an arrow. They are fairly expensive, but well worth the price. Representatives of the organizations will visit the area and site the signs at strategic points. There is a minimum fee, for about six signs, with an additional charge for any further ones.

Local radio stations

It is worth while to contact local radio stations, which are very good about giving information, usually on the Saturday, about local flower festivals. This is a superb form of advertising as it is often picked up by motorists on their car radios when they are out on day trips and they will sometimes deviate from their planned route to go to the festival.

Television

If the festival is a large one it is worth while trying to find some famous person to come to it and to make sure that some television station knows. If the television cameras are there photographing the VIP your publicity is assured!

Local press

A member of the publicity team must go and talk to the local press and describe the festival which is being planned. If there is a special feature or exhibition, talk about it, and suggest photographs well in advance of the festival. The problem about photographing the actual staging is that by that time it is too late for the current week's edition of the local newspaper. If, therefore, you are having a famous visitor, plug that fact; or try to get the press interested in the organizers; photographs of the chairman and the artistic director, if they are known in the area, all help.

A petal collage always creates enormous interest on the part of the press, and for that reason is well worth the effort involved. The staging of the collage starts early in festival week, so that a little mock-up with some of the workers is invaluable! A good publicity officer ought to be able to get the writter of the woman's page of the local paper interested. If the editor of that page were visited she might well make a feature of the work involved.

The committee should pay to have an advertisement inserted in the local paper. There is often a page on which forthcoming local events are described, and this page is read by most people who take the paper.

National press

Every effort should be made to get a large festival into the national press. The St Albans Abbey Festival in 1977 was featured in a large picture in *The Times* and this undoubtedly brought in visitors from a very wide area.

Travel agencies, tourist boards and hotels

If the festival is in or near to a big town, it is well worth giving pamphlets and other information to local hotels and also to travel agencies and tourist boards. A travel agency or tourist board which arranges sight-seeing tours will sometimes include a flower festival in the itinerary, and with this in mind a member of the publicity team should visit these organizations several months beforehand.

Women's Institutes, Townswomen's Guilds and Derby and Joan clubs

All these organizations, having outings in view, may be interested to hear of a flower festival, so write to them about six months in advance. They will want to know about catering arrangements – Derby and Joan Clubs will want to know exactly what kind of meals are available – and also – a vital piece of information! – about lavatory accommodation.

Diocesan Office and other churches

The Diocesan Office should be given the date of the festival as soon as it has been fixed. There is usually a diocesan magazine, or at least a leaflet, in which the date can be inserted, thus giving early notice to other churches which may have festivals in mind and will not want them to coincide. To have festivals in neighbouring churches at the same time is disastrous.

About two weeks before the festival pamphlets should be delivered to the local churches of all denominations with the request that they be displayed. Also ask the local clergy to give out in church details of the festival the week before it opens. If they do so at each service this is an excellent form of publicity.

12

Flower Festivals: From Viewing Day to Festival Week

VIEWING DAY

The committee must fix a day about two months before the flower festival when the church is open and the flower arrangers come to view it and to be given details of the festival. If it is a large festival it is as well to have two sessions, morning and afternoon, with a break for lunch. Viewing day is very important. If the organizers give time to welcome and listen to the helpers, it will set the whole tone of the festival. If everyone is happy at the beginning, they will still be happy at the end.

The incumbent will want to be at both sessions to welcome the visitors, to explain why the festival is being staged and to introduce the chairman of the committee, the artistic director and the secretary. The artistic director will then explain exactly what the festival scheme is and take the visitors round the whole church. A large plan of the building should be displayed on an easel where it is plainly visible. Every position for flowers should be shown numbered on it, so that the director can explain it.

It is important for the artistic director to encourage the visitors to supply as many garden flowers as possible and to explain what a flower pool (see Chapter 4) is. It is a very important part of a festival. There will be some people working on large flower arrangements who will want the church to supply flowers, and the secretary, who will be with the artistic director, will take down details of their requests. It is much better for the church to buy flowers from one local supplier than to leave it to each flower arranger to buy individually, a course which will enormously increase expenditure. There may be flower arrangers who will want the church to supply pedestals and containers: a careful list must be kept of requests of this sort.

Most flower festivals are dependent on outside help and the church must express its gratitude by thoroughly caring for these friends. On viewing day there must be tea or coffee available, and it is very much appreciated if during staging day refreshments are supplied. I remember one festival where there was a ploughman's lunch in the vestry, and it made all the difference. If the committee is able to make catering arrangements, information about them should be given out on viewing day.

Time should be given for each flower arranger to talk to the artistic director so that she can explain exactly the sort of arrangement which she has planned, including the overall size and the colouring. Some flower arrangers ask a great many questions on viewing day. They want to know the precise size, shape and type of arrangement or pedestal, window cill or other position which they are filling. My view is that the director's role is to give the exact colouring — a scheme is ruined if someone deviates from this — and an indication as to size. If there are pillar arrangements or pedestals or flower balls which need to be uniform in size, it is a good plan to have an example of each on viewing day and to keep a firm eye on staging day to make sure that the arrangements remain similar. There are, however, many other types of arrangement which, provided that the colouring is right, should express the individual arranger's taste and style. Flower arranging is, after all, an art, and the last thing a festival wants is rows of arrangements all alike.

Not everyone agrees with this view. I was interrogated at a large festival by a very fierce lady who wanted me to give an exact 'design' for a large window cill. I explained the colouring which I wanted, but I told her that I felt that she should plan her own scheme in this area. 'Are you the director?' she asked. 'Yes, I am' I replied. 'Well, in that case I suggest you direct!' Well, I did, and re-allocated the window cill to a brilliant man flower arranger, who filled it with glorious lilies and foliage quite beyond anything which I had envisaged. It was, of course, a show stopper!

It is useful at this time for the artistic director to have a notebook handy to jot down comments and ideas from the visiting flower arrangers, and in particular to make a note of any nervous helper. On staging day the director can then be at hand to help in a tactful way. I have had very inexperienced 'young wives' who with a little help and encouragement produced the most spectacular garlands at a festival although they were clueless and frightened at the beginning.

THE FLOWER POOL

Flower pools have already been mentioned in chapter 4, but when one is planning a flower festival the organization of the flower pool will be rather different from that at other times. Not only will the pool include flowers and foliage picked from gardens, but, because of the need for flowers in specially selected colours, it will also be necessary to purchase a certain amount of material. To ensure that the operation runs smoothly the organization of the pool will need at least two people, and in the case of a cathedral many more.

The great thing about flower pool personnel is that the best people for the job are not necessarily flower arrangers at all; keen gardeners are excellent, or practical housewives with some knowledge of plant material — in other words, the flower pool is a good way of using volunteers who do not want to be flower arrangers.

Methods of obtaining flowers

Immediately after viewing day, when it will have been possible to obtain a good idea of the flower arrangers' requirements, the flower pool organization should check on local gardens and ask their owners whether they are prepared to pick flowers for the festival and roughly what sort will be available. If the festival is in a cathedral, letters should be written to the owners of all the houses in the diocese with large gardens asking them for flowers. Letters from those answering in the affirmative should be filed and contact should be renewed with them about a month before the festival, inquiring about suitable times for collection. Sometimes flowers have to be picked by members of the flower pool organization, as well as collected, so that obtaining the flowers can be a very time-consuming operation. When gardens are able to provide a lot of flowers, offers of the use of estate cars or vans are invaluable.

Buying flowers

From the requests received on viewing day the secretary will have compiled a list of the flowers which will have to be purchased. The artistic director will also have requirements. All flowers to be bought will have to be carefully listed in colours and varieties and the festival committee will appoint someone to buy all the necessary material. Most churches have a local supplier from whom they buy throughout the year, and this will generally be the best source. Some local nurseries will not only supply the church with flowers but will deliver the material in buckets which they will lend for the duration of the festival.

Hedgerow and other wild material

Depending on the time of year, there is a lot of excellent material to be had free (See page 24). A member of the flower pool organization should be prepared to go and pick what is needed and bring it straight into the church to be carefully conditioned: likewise any interesting material from vegetable gardens.

Receiving and conditioning flowers

A corner of the church must be earmarked for the flower pool. Polythene sheeting should be laid down, on which will be put endless buckets, baby baths and other large utensils filled with water. You will need twice as many containers as you think! Not all churches have a water supply laid on. Where a church has no water it is essential to have a hosepipe to bring water into the building from a source nearby.

As the material is brought into the church there should be at least two people on duty to receive it, condition it, and plunge it into water. Remember that some material will need boiling water treatment, so have an electric kettle handy.

It saves time if the material is sorted into colours at an early stage. Any flowers which have been specially ordered should be put into buckets and labelled and kept separately.

Throughout the staging period there must always be someone on duty at the flower pool, partly to make sure that all the best stuff does not go all at once to one person — I am sorry to say that florists are very greedy when confronted with buckets of 'goodies' — and partly because as flower arrangers finish their work they usually give their spare material to the pool and it must be put into water immediately. It is horrifying to see dying material laying about the church-yard simply because there have been no buckets available. If the festival takes place at a hot time of the year, the organizers of the flower pool should expect to supply from the leftovers replenishments to be carefully tended and kept in a cool place.

Filling and spraying

When the flower arrangments are complete all the vases must, throughout the festival, be topped up at least once a day and every arrangement must be sprayed with an atomizer. The material will last provided that it is properly conditioned and cared for in this way. I have worked at several festivals in high summer where no replenishments have been

14   Window cill arrangement of mixed spring flowers at St Mary Magdalene,
Whipsnade

15 Wall plaque and garland of spring flowers at St Mary Magdalene, Whipsnade.
The garland includes polyanthus 'retaining roots' (see page 63)

16   Cow parsley and euphorbia arranged in a silver cup

17 Flower festival at St John the Baptist, Stanbridge. Flowers arranged to fit into a niche

18 Mary Magdalene, Whipsnade. An arrangement of dried material in grey, pinks, mauves and brown (glycerined beech)

19 St Albans Abbey flower festival. Detail of one panel of the petal collage. For details, see page 99

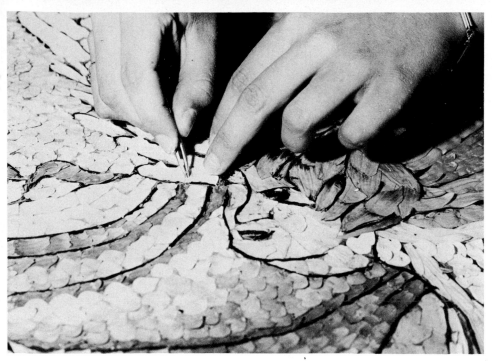

20 St Albans Abbey flower festival. Planning petals for the collage

21 Arum lilies arranged with natural foliage and chlorophytum at the parish church of St Leonard, Flamstead

22   Spring flowers arranged in a copper urn at St Leonard's church, Flamstead.
For details, see page 66

needed. Tall men are excellent for topping up and spraying. If a pedestal has a number of cones care must be taken that none are missed. Garlands, pillar arrangements and flower balls in particular need good spraying.

FESTIVAL WEEK: STAGING

We now come to the week of the festival, and the 'staging' of it, that term being used to describe the period during which the church is decorated with flowers and any special exhibitions are mounted. If the festival is to be opened to the public on Thursday evening, staging usually starts on Wednesday evening and continues through Thursday until about 4.00 pm. Now we come to the daily tasks of the week itself.

Monday

1   Organization of all mechanics, a vitally important task. The mechanics for garlands, flower balls, pillar tops, etc., should all be made and positioned.

2   All pedestals and containers provided by the church should be placed in position filled with chicken wire.

3   The secretary must give all the positions the numbers which will have been allocated to them on the artistic director's plan.

4   Check that there are enough watering cans, small florist's cans with long spouts, and atomizers.

5   Have ready stub wires, polythene bags, reel wire, string, stub scissors, wirecutters and spare dust sheets.

6   If possible, have available a large water butt or similar container for water.

Tuesday

In the evening:

1   Fill all containers — baby baths, buckets, etc — needed for soaking *Oasis*.

2   Fill the water butt so that the flower arrangers can easily fill containers from it. This should be inside the building.

Wednesday morning

Start soaking the *Oasis*.

Wednesday evening and Thursday

The secretary must be present throughout these two days of staging to check with each flower arranger her allotted space and to help generally. The artistic director will also be present to help and advise, and generally the chairman is also available for most of the time.

I have said earlier, but it is worth repeating here, that refreshments for helpers should be available during the staging day, and are much appreciated.

When staging is completed the church should be cleared ready to receive the public. It is important at this point to re-organize the flower pool into colours and to put it into a corner where it will not be seen by visitors. Any replenishments needed during the festival will come from the pool.

All vases and cones should be topped up and all arrangements sprayed, and when these jobs are completed there comes the magic moment when the organizers can stand back and see the results of their year's work. Even if there have had to be compromises with the design, perhaps due to bad weather and a dearth of flowers, this is still a tremendously exciting time.

Preview

Some churches arrange a preview as a form of publicity before the festival is opened to the public. The preview takes place during the evening before opening day. Very often it takes the form of a wine and cheese party or a buffet supper. A number of well-known local people — such as the Lord Lieutenant, the Chairman of the County Council, mayors, leaders of district councils and so on — are invited and of course are not asked to pay for their tickets; but members of the general public are asked on the basis that they pay for admission. The refreshments are usually provided in a hall near the church, or in a large house if there is a kind friend of the church who will lend one for this purpose. The visitors are then able to go round the church in a leisurely way admiring the exhibits in uncrowded conditions: indeed, if they are quite numerous, it may be better to arrange for them to go round at intervals in two or three separate parties.

A preview does, of course, mean a lot of extra work for those members of the festival committee concerned with catering, and also those dealing with publicity, who will be responsible for having tickets printed and for sending out invitations. It is, however, a good way of getting the festival off to a flying start.

13

Flower Festivals: Special Exhibits and Children's Corner

PETAL COLLAGE

If the committee decides to have a special exhibit at the flower festival, one of the most dramatic which it can choose is a petal collage. This has its origins in the ancient custom of well-dressing, which is particularly associated with Derbyshire. It is recorded as early as 1350, then seems to have fallen into disuse, but was revived in 1615.

Griselda Blaikiston, who has been concerned with many flower festivals in the Winchester areas, hit upon the brilliant notion of expanding the original rather naive idea of the well-dressing into a more sophisticated, carefully planned collage, composed primarily of petals but including other plant material. Many churches successfully copied her idea, including St Albans Abbey (photograph 19). If the instructions are followed and some time and trouble is taken to organize the collage team, the making of the collage is not so difficult as it sounds.

There is, of course, work for one or two people before the festival, and teams are needed on the day, but the great advantage is that the workers can be of all ages. 'Senior citizens' are excellent, as are children of about 7–12 years old: and none of them need be flower arrangers, so that it is a lovely way of interesting the entire neighbourhood. The other great advantage is that the publicity team love it. The press nearly always features the collage several days in advance of the festival. I have no doubt that at those festivals at which I have worked and which have included a petal collage the number of visitors has been far greater than is normal.

The construction of the collage calls for various and considerable skills, enormous industry in assembling the petal material, disciplined teamwork in the face of a tight time schedule, patience and concentration by the team members, and constant overall artistic direction, not by the festival's artistic director, but by someone who has the requisite knowledge and can give her whole time to the task of supervision on the day on which the picture is built up.

The base

The first person whom the committee will need to find is a competent, albeit amateur, carpenter, because the collage has as its base a bed of damp potter's clay about one inch deep contained within a wooden frame. Because the damp clay is very heavy, and the completed picture will have to be moved from a horizontal to a vertical position, the frame must be strong and rigid. The exact size of the collage is a matter for the committee to decide, but it must be large enough to form a striking exhibit and therefore cannot well be less tham 4ft high and 2ft 6in wide. In a cathedral or large church it may be possible to be more enterprinsing and have, not a single picture, but a triptych, as we did at the St Albans Abbey Flower Festival in 1977.

The first step is to make a wooden frame of the required size. To this is fixed a piece of plasterboard or similar material. This must be strong, yet sufficiently thin for it to be possible to hammer one-inch nails, through it, set all over it and about one inch apart from one another, so protruding that when the frame is turned onto its back one is faced with a bed of nails. When the bed of nails has been formed, the back of the frame is further strengthened with cross-battens. The frame is now ready to receive the clay.

It will be necessary to work out the quantity of potter's clay required for the particular frame which has been constructed. Many art colleges will lend clay. The purpose of the nails is to hold the clay in place, but the tips of the nails must be just covered. It is essential to have clay in reserve and not to run short.

The clay is mixed with water so as to give it the consistency of sticky, but not too liquid, mud, akin to plasticene. It is essential at all stages of the making of the picture to keep the clay thoroughly damp with a florist's spray, remembering that the petals have to adhere to it. During the making of the picture it may be found necessary to add clay at the edges, so throughout the process a pail of soft clay must be immediately to hand.

The clay, mixed to the right consistency, is poured onto the bed of nails so as just to cover them. Before starting this operation the frame must be placed on a strong and steady trestle or similar table as near as possible to the place where the collage is to be displayed. This is important, because, as I have said, the clay is very heavy; so when complete the collage, itself fragile, is difficult to move, and the shorter the distance which it has to be moved the better. At least three people will be needed to lift it from the horizontal to the vertical, and it goes without saying that the table or other support upon which it is going to be displayed must be substantial, and that the collage must be so positioned on it that it cannot shift.

It is also vital that the working table is absolutely level, and that when the clay is poured into the frame a completely flat surface is achieved. When the frame has been filled with clay, work on the building up of the picture can begin.

Making the picture

Obviously the committee will decide at an early stage what is to be the subject of the collage. It will usually be a subject associated with the building or the place. When in our village, Flamstead, we had a flower festival in 1973, an attractive stained glass window was chosen as a subject (see photograph 17). At St Albans Abbey the triptych portrayed the saint's martyrdom.

Whatever subject is chosen, an artist must prepare in the appropriate colours the design which is to be copied in petals. Both colouring and design must be clear and simple. During the making of the collage the design – generally called the 'cartoon' – must be affixed (probably with adhesive tape) to a wall or large blackboard – remember that the cartoon will be the same size as the collage – so that those working on the collage can easily see and follow it.

The designer of the cartoon must be a competent, but need not be a very experienced, artist. The cartoon for the collage at Flamstead was drawn by an 'A' level art student and her college of art was most helpful in every way. They in fact lent us the clay.

The cartoon is traced onto greaseproof paper. Having regard to its size, it is easier from the point of view of transferring it to the clay (the next step) to trace it in two pieces, but they must join exactly.

Assuming that the festival is to open on Thursday evening, and that the collage must be finished by then, the outline of the picture must be put onto the clay on Wednesday. The tracing is laid on the bed of clay and the outlines of the picture are transferred to it by prick marks, made with a toothpick or similar small sharp instrument through the tracing. The marks must be sufficiently close together to preserve the outlines accurately. Bootlace seaweed is then pressed into the outlines so that it is level with the surface of the clay. If the tracing is done in two halves, prick out the first half, take off the tracing, and apply the seaweed. Then repeat the process with the other half. A bucketful of seaweed is needed, and one requires both the very fine and the thicker variety, as it will be desirable to make some outlines thicker than others.

Skilful use can be made of 'hooks' etc in the weed in delineating the outline. Remember that every part of the picture must be carefully outlined. The weed must be kept damp before use. The kind needed can be found in Cornwall and on the west coast of Scotland at low tide. Provided that it is kept damp, it can if need be collected some time before the festival. It is much the best material for outlines but, if it is quite impossible to procure it, black wool can be used instead.

On the basis that the picture has been completely traced in outline in seaweed or wool on Wednesday, work on filling in the picture with petals must begin early on Thursday, not later than 10.00 am if the collage is 4ft x 2ft 6in and is to be finished by 6.00 pm. The work is carried out by teams of four people working in shifts, each team working for two hours at a stretch, with a new team waiting to take cver the moment a shift has finished. The 'artists' do not need to have any particular skill provided that they have good concentration and are neat-fingered. They have the cartoon in front of them to copy and the eagle-eyed collage director there to guide them when necessary.

It is essential that each person working on the picture should be provided with:

A chair or stool
At least four plastic dishes in which to put petals
About four plastic or wooden cocktail sticks
A pair of nail scissors
A pair of eyebrow tweezers with square ends

It will also be necessary to have some small tables upon which to put the dishes of petals which are being used, and there must be a flower spray for moistening the clay if it shows signs of becoming too dry so that the petals do not adhere properly to it. There is bound to be a good deal of mess, so there should be dust sheets or newspaper to protect the floor. Each worker should also be provided with a pail of clean water and a towel so that she can wash her hands if necessary.

One of the principal skills in planning the collage is the selection of the petals, and the grading of them not only into colours but also into sizes, as the effect of shading can often be achieved by the careful arrangement of petals of the same type and colour of flower or foliage but graduated in size. So that the building up of the picture can continue without interruption the director must know precisely what she wants, and this will involve trying out arrangements of petals in advance, using for this purpose a small board covered with clay. The director will also have to estimate the quantities of different petals required. A great quantity of flowers in needed, especially for the background.

Suitable flowers

Provided that the surface is kept moist — but not too wet — by regular spraying with an atomizer, it is remarkable how long the collage will retain its freshness — even for ten days or more. To some extent, however, the time for which it lasts depends upon the flowers used. Dahlias, for example, are not very satisfactory and should therefore be avoided.

If at first reading the instructions for making the collage sound too daunting, do think again! The task is not as complicated as it sounds and the project is a fascinating one which, as I have said, greatly increases the number of visitors to the festival. If you are in Derbyshire, find out from the local Tourist Board office when the well-dressings take place and see them if you can. While a petal collage is, as I have explained, a far more sophisticated thing, the well-dressings will help you enormously in visualizing the finished picture.

CHILDREN'S CORNER

Children are eager to help at flower festivals and they like to be responsible for some special feature. They enjoy bringing their proud relations to show them their own particular project. Amongst Sunday school children of reasonable age, Brownies and local schoolchildren, it is possible to find willing and very often original helpers. There are many sorts of decorations for children to do. The following are a few ideas.

Kneelers

In several churches where I have worked the children have made imitation 'kneelers' out of flowers. Each child or group of children was provided with a seed tray to be filled with either damp sand or *Oasis*, into which the children pushed the heads of flowers so as to form a design. Very often they made a background of flat leaves and then made the design on that. It is fascinating how talented small children can be, producing beautiful designs with no apparent help from grown-ups!

The 'kneelers' were placed together lengthwise on either side of the chancel so as make bright strips of colour leading up to the alter. In another church instead of 'kneelers' the same mechanics were used to make a 'carpet' in front of the altar. Another place where a carpet could be 'laid' would be the porch. Narrow strips on either side leading up to the door would be enchanting.

Fonts

Fonts are very often surrounded by steps. These can be decorated by children to give the effect of beds of flowers simply by putting on the steps tins containing *Oasis* and filling them with flowers.

Easter garden

At an Easter flower festival the obvious thing for children to make is an Easter garden (see page 75).

Pew ends and garlands

Older children if they are well supervised can easily make garlands. Equally, if given a pattern, they can do 'pew ends'. It would be very suitable if these could be incorporated in the children's corner.

Petal collage

The petal collage described on pages 100-103 provides an admirable opportunity for children. Their nimble little fingers are ideal for the delicate work involved. Children aged from about 8-12 are perfect for this work, provided that they are prepared to do a two-hour stretch. My experience is that at first they think that this is too long, but the good ones become so entranced that at the end of that time they have to be prized out of their places.

Glossary

Altar frontal or hangings covering for the front of the altar (communion table)

Arrangement flowers arranged in any kind of container

Arrangers' cupboard cupboard used to store equipment for flower arranging

Atomizer a fine spray used for freshening arrangements

Candle cup metal cup which fits into the top of a candlestick and hold *Oasis* or water

Conditioning preparation of plant material

Cone metal or plastic container for water used to give height to shorter flowers

Construction upright wooden or metal pole to which a series of containers is affixed

Container any utensil which holds water or *Oasis*

Equipment the basic tools and materials (often called 'the mechanics') used in flower arranging

Face large leaves or flowers placed in the centre of an arrangement to provide a focal point

Florist church flower arranger

Flower balls balls or flowers suspended, eg, in arches

Flower festival occasion when a church is specially decorated with flowers and open to the public

Flower pool central supply of flowers upon which flower arrangers can draw

Flower rota signifies the system whereby duties are allotted to flower guild members

Focal point the central point of a flower arrangement

Garland a strip of flowers, used horizontally, vertically or as an arc or circlet

Group large pedestal arrangement

Mechanics the equipment needed in flower arranging

Oasis an artificial substance which holds moisture

Petal collage a picture made primarily from petals

Pew end an arrangement to hang on the end of a pew

Pin-holder metal base with protruding spikes
Plaque arrangement to be hung on a wall
Reel wire silver or brown florist's wire wound on a reel
Spray see atomizer
Staging the period before a flower festival during which the building is being decorated
Strippers gadget to strip off thorns or leaves
Stub scissors scissors for cutting wire and plant material
Stub wires wires supplied in bundles of varying gauges and lengths

Further Reading

Best, Margaret and Godfrey, *The Miniature Flower Arrangement Book*, Arlington Books

Hay, Roy, and Synge, Patrick M., *Dictionary of Garden Plants in Colour*, Michael Joseph, 1969

Macqueen, Sheila, *Complete Flower Arranging*, Hyperion Books, Ward Lock Ltd, in association with Peter Crawley, 1979

Macqueen, Sheila, *Flower Arranging from your Garden*, Hyperion Books, Ward Lock Ltd, in association with Peter Crawley, 1977

Oxford Book of Garden Flowers, Oxford University Press, 1963

Oxford Book of Wild Flowers, Oxford University Press, 1976

Piercy, Harold, *The Constance Spry Book of Flower Arranging*, Sundial Publications, 1979

Taylor, Jean, *Plants and Flowers for Lasting Decoration*, Batsford, 1981

For information on local flower clubs contact N.A.F.A.S, 21A Denbigh Street, London SW1.

Index